What people are saying about

Mindfulness Based Living Course

It is with great pleasure that I recommend this introduction to mindfulness written by Heather and Choden. The world is being swamped by books and articles on this topic so readers may wonder why yet another? The reason is simple – this is a practical DIY for those who might be interested in the Mindfulness Based Living Course which is offered by the Mindfulness Association. I know that hundreds of people have done and benefitted from this course so feel confident in suggesting that many more people, including you, will benefit from it.

Rob Nairn, author of *Diamond Mind: A Psychology of Meditation*

This user-friendly workbook connects mindfulness, warm-heartedness, and insight – plus offers many practical tools for daily life. Reading it feels like being with a wise and encouraging friend. The writing is clear and direct, and comes from world-class mindfulness teachers. A wonderful resource!

Rick Hanson, PhD, author of *Buddha's Brain: The Practical Neuroscience of Happiness, Love, and Wisdom*

T0159070

Mindfulness Based Living Course

Eight Week Mindfulness Course

Mindfulness Based Living Course

Eight Week Mindfulness Course

Choden & Heather Regan-Addis

BOOKS

Winchester, UK
Washington, USA

First published by O-Books, 2018
O-Books is an imprint of John Hunt Publishing Ltd., 3 East St., Alresford,
Hampshire SO24 9EE, UK
office1@jhpbooks.net
www.johnhuntpublishing.com

For distributor details and how to order please visit the 'Ordering' section on our website.

ISBN: 978 1 78535 832 6
978 1 78535 840 1 (ebook)
Library of Congress Control Number: 2017950790

A CIP catalogue record for this book is available from the British Library.

Design: Stuart Davies

Printed and bound by CPI Group (UK) Ltd, Croydon, CR0 4YY, UK

Contents

Dedication

For our friend and teacher

Rob Nairn

without whom this MBLC course would not be possible

Developed by Mindfulness Association Ltd

Acknowledgements

Choden and Heather have many people to thank for their advice, support and encouragement. We are truly fortunate and grateful to our teachers, family and friends. We would like to thank our teacher and patron of the Mindfulness Association Choje Lama Yeshe Losal Rinpoche for his teaching, advice and constant support for the Mindfulness Association and for us both personally. Your advice to include kindness, compassion and appreciation in the MBLC curriculum was transformative for many of our MBLC students. We would also like to thank our friend, teacher and founder of the Mindfulness Association, Rob Nairn, for his support and friendship and for his gift of the systematic and effective Mindfulness training on which the MBLC is based. He has guided us, and his students past many of the obstacles that can stand in the way of an effective Mindfulness practice. We would also like to thank Professor Paul Gilbert, who is patron of the Mindfulness Association, for his support and advice in the field of evolutionary psychology. Thanks also goes to Norton Bertram-Smith and Vin Harris as founding Directors of the Mindfulness Association for their business acumen, friendship and support for the Mindfulness Association and for us both personally. We would also like to thank the Mindfulness Association tutor team for their friendship, advice and support in the ongoing teaching and development of the Mindfulness curriculum and our HQ team for their friendship and support. We would like to give special thanks to Isabel Coughlin for so diligently proofreading the final draft of the book. Thanks to Heather Grace Bond who set up the MBLC guided audio apps on Android and Apple. Thanks also to Pixel8 in Manchester for the graphic design of the book cover. Finally, we would like to thank our many course participants over the years for their engagement with the Mindfulness curriculum as it has developed.

Heather's acknowledgements: I would particularly like to thank my husband Mark and my daughter Jenny for their love and support and for putting up with my many absences while I am away teaching. I love you both very much.

We hope that this book will help to bring freedom from the conditioning that governs and limits our lives so that our human potential to bring benefit to the world can flourish.

Introduction

This book is intended for everyone – everyone who has ruminated on the past over mistakes made and opportunities lost; everyone who has found themselves compulsively worrying about a future scenario that may never happen; everyone who has missed the alive-ness of this moment while lost in thinking; and everyone who has found themselves astonished by a beautiful view or immersed in a moment of loving connection, and wished they had more moments like this in their lives.

The authors of this book have taught the practice of Mindfulness and Compassion to hundreds of people and we have seen how these practices can transform people's lives. We have seen how Mindfulness opens up an inner space of awareness, in which we are less caught in the ups and downs of life, and where we learn to build a different relationship with ourselves – one in which we are more content, because we are making less demands on ourselves; less reactive, because we are learning to accept what comes up in our experience; and more open and curious about the unfolding experience of our lives, because we see life as a unique process of emergence rather than as a relentless struggle to survive.

This is the gift of Mindfulness.

In this book we want to share this gift with you and offer simple tools for making Mindfulness an ongoing part of your life experience. Before doing so, we would like to present a short history of secular Mindfulness and our particular place in this emerging modern phenomenon.

A Short History of Secular Mindfulness

The practice of Mindfulness is found in many spiritual traditions, but the majority of Mindfulness-based courses now available in the West, including the one in this book, are derived from

Buddhism.

The teachings of the Buddha were first written down in a language called Pali from which the word 'sati' has been translated as into English as 'Mindfulness'. The word 'sati' also has the connotation of 'remembrance' or 'recollectedness', which is a key aspect in Mindfulness practice. We can all be present, but the problem is that we all too easily forget to be present, and so the skills of 'remembering' to be present and 'recollecting' our intention to be present are important.

The idea of a secular (non-religious) Mindfulness eight-week course was first introduced to the West by Jon Kabat-Zinn in the early 1980s, as a way of dealing with chronic conditions in a health care context. He developed a program called *Mindfulness Based Stress Reduction* (MBSR) and wrote his book *Full Catastrophe Living* (1990) about this program. From the beginning Jon Kabat-Zinn took an evidence-based approach to his Mindfulness training, conducting research into its effectiveness. This has resulted in a large and ever-growing evidence base of research studies, which indicate that MBSR is effective in enabling people to cope better with conditions, such as chronic pain, diabetes and heart disease. More importantly, this research indicates that Mindfulness practice enables people to flourish in their lives and find greater physical and mental well-being.

Much of this research asks people to fill in a questionnaire before they begin a Mindfulness course. These questionnaires measure things such as well-being, stress levels, self-compassion and Mindfulness. Then after completing the Mindfulness course, people fill in the questionnaires again and a statistical analysis is done to measure any significant changes. Other research involves taking saliva samples and testing for antibodies, before and after a Mindfulness course. This research has shown that stress levels were reduced and immune response was improved after the course. Also, brain scans have shown changes in brain activity after a Mindfulness course.

These changes have been detected after only an eight-week long course in Mindfulness, with participants attending weekly classes and practising Mindfulness for 45 minutes a day for 6 days a week. A measurable change for the better can be seen in only eight weeks. This is very encouraging for the novice Mindfulness practitioner. However, research consistently shows that those participants who do the recommended 45 minutes, 6 days a week benefit far more than those who do less practice. So, reading and learning about Mindfulness is not enough; it is important to practise – this is the focus of our book.

Building on MBSR, in the mid-1990s Mark Williams, John Teasdale and Zindel Segal were looking for a group therapy that could be used to help those in remission from depression not to relapse. They developed Mindfulness-Based Cognitive Therapy (MBCT), an eight-week Mindfulness course, which is derived from Jon Kabat-Zinn's MBSR, but also includes exercises from Cognitive Behavioural Psychotherapy. They wrote about this program in their book *Mindfulness-Based Cognitive Therapy for Depression* (2002). This course is aimed at reducing people's habits of ruminative thinking, where they go over and over the same problem in their minds, trying to find a solution, but instead causing low mood and triggering further bouts of depression.

There is good evidence from randomised control trials that MBCT can help people who have been depressed three or more times from relapsing again. As a result of this research the UK National Institute for Health and Care Excellence (NICE) recommends MBCT for this client group. MBCT is now used extensively in the National Health Service in the UK, primarily in the field of mental health.

Rob Nairn and the Mindfulness Association

Rob Nairn is a meditation teacher within the Tibetan Buddhist tradition. He was first asked to teach meditation by the Dalai Lama – a good recommendation!

Since then Rob has been teaching meditation for over forty years. When Rob teaches he uses psychological language as opposed to Buddhist terminology to make teachings on meditation accessible to Westerners. He teaches with an intimate knowledge of the workings of the human mind, derived from his own practice and from the many meditation masters with whom he has studied. He has the ability to help his students navigate the many subtle obstacles to an effective meditation practice. Rob's book *Diamond Mind: A Psychology of Meditation* (2001) describes his methodical and insightful approach to teaching meditation.

In 2008 Rob developed and led his first systematic and progressive training in Mindfulness, over three weekends and a weeklong retreat, assisted by the authors: Choden and Heather. This course formed the basis for the Mindfulness Association's (MA's) four weekend Mindfulness training. This course is now taught all over the UK and in Ireland, Iceland, South Africa, Belgium, Italy, Spain and Poland.

Rob and the MA team then went on to develop a three-weekend training in Compassion, drawing upon a fusion of the Mahayana Buddhist approach to compassion and the scientific approach, grounded in evolutionary psychology and neuroscience, that was pioneered by Professor Paul Gilbert. Paul is now a patron of the MA, and he and Choden have written a book entitled *Mindful Compassion* (2013).

The MA team then developed a three-weekend training in Insight. This involves an exploration of the subtle, unseen forces that lock us into limiting habitual patterns. It is based on the foundation of stability that comes from Mindfulness training and the kindness and acceptance that comes from Compassion training.

Therefore, the MA is able to provide a three-year progressive training in Mindfulness, Compassion and Insight for people to develop a deep and effective meditation practice.

Our other patron is Choje Lama Yeshe Rinpoche, who is the abbot of Samye Ling Tibetan centre and a meditation master, having completed twelve years of solitary meditation retreat. He advised the MA team to include kindness and compassion in our Mindfulness trainings right from the beginning, which we have done. This is one of the features that distinguishes the MA's Mindfulness training from the other secular Mindfulness trainings, in particular MBSR and MBCT.

The Mindfulness, Compassion and Insight trainings offered by the MA form the basis for collaboration with the University of Aberdeen, in the delivery of their MSc in Mindfulness Studies. This MSc started in 2010 and is currently recruiting its ninth cohort of students, regularly attracting over 50 new students per year with around 120 students currently in the program. The main focus of this MSc is the application of Mindfulness practice to different professional contexts, including mental and physical health care, social work, education and training, business and coaching. This MSc takes a social science research approach, which contrasts with the clinical model used for the other UK MSc courses that teach MBSR and MBCT.

The Mindfulness Based Living Course (MBLC), which is the basis for this book, is derived mainly from the MA's Mindfulness training, but also includes some theory and practices from the MA's Compassion training. The course is made up of an introductory session, eight weekly sessions and a follow-up session afterwards.

Practicalities

This book takes you through the Mindfulness Based Living Course (MBLC) in a step-by-step way. Although it is written in a self-help style, with spaces to make notes of your experience of doing the practices, our intention is that this book is either an encouragement to do a mindfulness training, or an accompaniment to such a training. One of the core principles of mindfulness is that it should be taught face-to-face by someone who embodies mindfulness, and ideally in group context with other like-minded learners. We have an experienced team of MBLC teachers who regularly run 8-week courses throughout the UK. For more information on the Mindfulness Association, the trainings we offer and our membership scheme see: www. mindfulnessassociation.net.

Guided audio of the practices of the MBLC course is available on the Mindfulness Association's free Mindfulness Based Living app, which is available from the Google Play store for Android devices and from the app store for iOS devices. The guided audio can also be streamed or downloaded from this web page: mindfulnessassociation.net/mblc-book.

Chapter 1

What is Mindfulness & Why Practise It?

Mindful Eating Exercise

Follow the Mindful Eating Exercise written out below or follow the guided audio.

Traditionally, several raisins are used for this exercise in mindful eating, but interesting alternatives are tangerines, a square of chocolate or a shortbread biscuit. To begin with, have the food resting in your hand and just see it, noticing how it looks, whether light reflects off its surface, the colours and textures that can be observed. Now feel the weight of it in your hand and notice how the contact feels between the food and your hand, and if the object is a tangerine, feel the process of peeling it. Spend some time smelling the food, what scent do you notice? Also, as you smell the food do you notice if anything happens in your mouth. Now place the food in your mouth and feel it resting on your tongue. Can you notice the feelings of contact between the food and your mouth? Do you notice any difference from how the food felt in your hand? What is happening in your mouth as the food rests there? Then take one bite into the food and notice what happens. Are there any textures and tastes that you notice? Slowly chew the food and notice how your experience of eating unfolds. Then swallow the food and see if it is possible to follow the passage of the food down the throat and notice how far you can feel it go. Notice whether there is any aftertaste in the mouth. Then mindfully eat a few more bits of the food, exploring the different senses of taste, smell, touch and sight. Take about 10 minutes in total to eat mindfully.

Write down here what you noticed about your experience:

_____

_____

_____

_____

_____

_____

Did you notice the weight, texture and feel of the food in your hand before you put it in your mouth? What did it smell like? How did it feel in your mouth and how did it taste? Is this your normal experience of eating?

For many people this exercise can be a revelation, because they realise how the rich and nourishing experience of eating is usually rushed and ignored. Usually we eat quickly and then swallow our food without savouring its taste and texture, so often caught up in thinking about something else. In this way we miss out on the simple delight of eating that is available to us through our senses if only we choose to pay attention.

In a similar way we live so much of our lives on automatic pilot, out of touch with our moment-by-moment experience and lost in thinking. A good example of this is driving a car or taking a bus. On arriving at our destination we might realise that we have noticed very little about our journey – the sights, smells and sounds along the way and instead we might see how we have been caught up in thinking or dreaming, listening to music on the radio, or immersed in the virtual reality of our phone. In doing this we are missing out on the richness of our lives, missing out on connecting with people around us and missing out on the insights that can arise from being in touch with our inner world.

Perhaps this wouldn't matter so much if we were thinking happy thoughts, but so often this is not the case. Mostly we get caught up in ruminating about our problems and worries, and in the process we become even more stressed and miserable. This is where Mindfulness can make a big difference to how we live our lives, so let's look at what Mindfulness is and why we might choose to practise it.

What is Mindfulness?

Mindfulness is a faculty that we already possess. It is not something that we need to import from the outside. It is like a muscle that we did not realise we had and that we have seldom used, so it is weak. Just as we can train a muscle by going to a gym, we can train the faculty of Mindfulness through doing practice. In short, this faculty needs to be recognised and then trained.

Rob Nairn describes Mindfulness as:

Knowing what is happening, while it is happening, without preference.

The key element in this definition is 'knowing'. This does not refer to conceptual knowing, but to a quality of simple awareness: we are aware of what is happening while it is happening. This might not seem like a big deal when we start, but the more we practise Mindfulness the more we realise that although what we experience is constantly changing, awareness does not change. More and more we learn to come to rest in this awareness and to relate to our lives from this place. When we do this we find a place of stability within ourselves that we can come to rely upon and trust. From this stability, insight naturally arises into what is happening within our minds and in life around us. In this way, we do less and see more.

The definition also illustrates that there are two aspects to Mindfulness training. The first is technique: *"Knowing what is happening, while it is happening"* and the second is attitude: *"without preference"*.

Technique

The technique is to stay present and be aware of what is happening both within our mind and the outer environment. Mindfulness is a way of being in touch with life directly as it emerges, unfolds and changes. This skill is deceptively simple but hard to practise. The mind very quickly drifts away from simple awareness of the present moment into thinking about things, and in this way we lose touch with the quality of knowing that lies at the heart of Mindfulness. For this reason we need methods to help us stay present.

In our approach we use a four-stage method:

- we learn to settle our jumpy 'monkey mind' through breathing and counting
- we bring ourselves more fully into the body through grounding
- we come to rest in the space of awareness that exists in and around our experience
- we use a neutral support (like sound or breath) to bring our attention back to this simple awareness of being present when it drifts away into thinking

This will be explored in more detail later, but right now the important point is to appreciate that we need a set of methods or techniques to help us train the mind. As many Buddhist teachers remark, it does not matter how many times our attention drifts away into thinking, the only important thing is to notice this and bring our attention back to the present – and for this we need a method.

Attitude

This second aspect is a crucial part of the training. If we practise the Mindfulness methods with a critical or judgmental attitude, we can end up being even more critical of ourselves – especially when we notice things in ourselves that are unpleasant or difficult. Acceptance lies at the heart of the attitude we are trying to cultivate. It means being OK with whatever is occurring within our minds, whether pleasant, unpleasant or boring – hence the phrase *"without preference"* in the definition above. This entails making space for difficult feelings and emotions and not getting caught up in reacting to them. As Rob Nairn so often says, "Nothing is wrong!" This statement points to something really important that lies at the heart of Mindfulness training: even if things feel bad and difficult we do not need to reject these feelings, because they are part of the richness of who we are as human beings. Through reading this book we hope that you will come to understand the far-reaching implications of Rob's statement and how it can transform your life.

Another important element of the attitude is cultivating warmth and kindness to what arises in our experience. We are not simply dispassionate and neutral to what we feel, but we learn to hold the inner movement of sensations and feelings with kindness. The meaning of kindness in this context is not judging ourselves for the experience we are having. This allows the mind to open up and not contract around difficult feelings. It is also a way of acknowledging what is right and well within our experience.

As Jon Kabat-Zinn states:

So long as we are breathing there is more right with us than is wrong with us.

11

This is reassuring as all of us reading this book are breathing!

Why Practise Mindfulness?

Mindfulness is an experiential process. It requires us to practise it rather than think about it too much. For this reason when we ask ourselves the question of why we might want to practise it, it is best to turn to our own experience for answers rather than get involved in a process of analytical thinking. In this respect, reflect on the following questions:

- How often do you do one thing while thinking about something else? Like washing the dishes while ruminating over an argument you had with a colleague.
- How often do you find yourself dwelling on the past or worrying about the future?
- How does it make you feel to live your life this way? Do you notice any feelings of conflict or stress or a drop in your mood?
- Would you like to find a different way of relating to your thoughts and emotions – one that is more accepting and less reactive?

This is the path of Mindfulness practice.

Some universal benefits to practising Mindfulness include:

- Appreciating the richness of the moment-by-moment experience rather than glossing over this as you race through your life on automatic pilot
- Becoming kinder and less critical towards yourself and others
- Becoming less reactive and so less likely to hurt yourself or others through destructive emotions like anger, jealousy and resentment
- Improving your relationships through being more present,

responsive and attentive to friends, loved ones, strangers, and even enemies

- Allowing your mind to become more settled and calm
- Enabling your inherent wisdom and compassion to emerge and enrich your everyday experience, so that you fulfil your potential as a human being

Key research findings on the benefits of Mindfulness practice are:

- It can enable us to cope with medical (physical and mental health) and non-medical problems
- It can help to reduce stress, anxiety and rumination
- It can help to increase empathy and self-compassion
- It can reduce emotional distress, increase positive states of mind and improve quality of life
- It can influence the brain, autonomic nervous system, stress hormones and the immune system in positive ways
- It can promote healthy eating and sleeping
- It can promote optimal health in mind, body, spirit and relationships

Chapter 2

Session One – Start Here and Now

Guided Reflection on Intention and Motivation

Spend a few minutes reflecting on the following questions and filling out the sections below. Try not to think too much about the answers, but just see what emerges without any expectations. Give time for a few answers to emerge, but also be OK if no answers come at the moment. You may find that answers to these questions arise at other times, such as when you are going to sleep, when you are washing up or when you are out walking. If this happens, make a note and write them down below later.

What is my intention or purpose in following the course in this book?

_____

_____

_____

How do I hope to benefit from it?

_____

_____

_____

How do I want it to change the way that I live my life?

_____

_____

_____

How do I want it to benefit the people in my life and in the world?

_____

_____

_____

What are my deepest hopes and aspirations in following this course?

_____

_____

_____

Can I express these in the form of a personal vision or aspiration, which communicates my wholehearted intention?

_____

_____

_____

If we lose our motivation to practise after a few weeks it can be useful to come back and look at these notes, to remind ourselves why it is that we want to practise Mindfulness.

It is important not to make our intention and motivation into a goal or an expectation, so that we are constantly measuring our progress against our desired outcomes. So once we clarify our intention and motivation, then let go of any aims or expectations and instead just follow the course and do the practices. Then review how it has gone when you get to the end of the course.

Intention, Motivation and Sharing

We use intention, motivation and sharing to frame each of our sessions of Mindfulness practice. We reflect on intention and motivation at the beginning of each session of practice, and we reflect on the benefits of our practice and share these benefits with others at the end of each session. So each session has a beginning, a middle and an end.

Intention

Reflecting on our intention sets our direction of travel. Before we do anything in life we start with an intention. When we are thirsty and want to drink a cup of tea, we first form an intention to make one. Similarly, at the beginning of a practice session we sit in our posture and form the intention to practise Mindfulness. We bring to mind the key elements of Mindfulness practice that have taken root in our own experience. Some examples of how we might express our intention are:

- To stay present
- To come back to being present when we notice that we are lost in thinking
- To be kind and gentle to ourselves during our practice

These are just suggestions and it is important that we make our intention our own – something that touches our heart and is meaningful to us. Intention drives change in the human mind and so reminding ourselves of our intention each time we practise helps us to stay on track with our aspiration: perhaps to be mindful, accepting and kind. For example, each time we notice that we are caught up in thinking, it is our intention to be present that reminds us to come back to the present moment. Each time we notice we are giving ourselves a hard time, because our minds are caught up in thinking again, it is our intention to be kind that reminds us to be gentle with ourselves.

Motivation

After reflecting on intention we then reflect on motivation. Whereas intention clarifies *what* we are doing, motivation clarifies *why* we are doing it. In this way motivation provides a broader context for our Mindfulness practice: why do I want to practise Mindfulness? Some examples of motivation are:

- Benefitting ourselves – for example becoming less stressed, sleeping better and feeling calmer
- Benefitting others – for example improving relationships with our loved ones and being less reactive with those people we find challenging

Again, these are just suggestions and it is important that we make our motivation personal and rooted in our own experience, so that it is meaningful to us. As our Mindfulness practice matures and we begin to see its potential to transform our lives, our motivation may change and develop. It might evolve, for example, from wanting to feel more calm and less stressed to aspiring to actualise our full potential as human beings and helping others to do the same.

Reflecting on our motivation each time we practise reminds us regularly of the importance of our Mindfulness practice in our lives. Over time it is our motivation that gets us out of bed in the morning and on to our cushion to meditate each day. It creates the force and impetus behind our practice.

Intention and motivation are like a bow and arrow. Intention is the arrow and motivation is the power behind the bow. First we point the arrow in the direction we wish it to go and then the muscles of the arm pull back the bow – the muscles are the power of motivation behind our intention. But just as we let go of the arrow once it is fired, in a similar way we let go of our intention once formed and trust that it will take us in the right direction. In this way we do not turn our intention into an expectation. We bring it to mind when we start to practise and then we let it go and trust in what happens.

Sharing

At the end of our session we take some time to reflect on the benefit we may have experienced from doing our Mindfulness practice. It is important to acknowledge that Mindfulness practice is an activity that we do that is beneficial to ourselves and to those around us, and to acknowledge how fortunate we are to be able to practise Mindfulness. Many people do not have this opportunity to train their minds. Then we cultivate a habit of generosity by sharing this benefit with others, in particular those who are less fortunate than we are. We make the wish that others may benefit from our Mindfulness practice. This practice of sharing counteracts the tendency to become self-absorbed and it encourages us to open up to a bigger space of awareness in which we acknowledge our connection with all living beings.

Posture Sitting in a Chair

Mindfulness practice involves placing both the mind and the body in an appropriate context that nurtures the emergence of awareness. We place the mind by setting our intention and motivation. We then place the body by paying close attention to our posture.

The body is a great ally in Mindfulness practice because it is always present, even though the mind wanders all over the place. For this reason we use the posture of the body as a container for holding the mind. Moreover, the posture of the body is a metaphor for our intention. It embodies the following qualities that we are aspiring to in our practice:

- Alert
- Open
- Grounded
- Dignified
- At ease, embodying kindness to ourselves

A useful metaphor for posture is imagining the body like a mountain, the breath like the wind and the mind like the sky.

Some people believe that it is important to sit on the floor on a cushion to meditate, but this is not true. Sitting on a chair is just as good an option. Choose a chair which is upright, for example a dining room chair, rather than an armchair. Place your feet flat upon the floor, roughly hip-width apart, with your thighs horizontal. To achieve this position, if you have long legs you may need to sit on a cushion or if you have short legs you can place a cushion or other support under your feet. Try not to lean against the back of the chair, sit a little away from it, so your back is self-supporting, straight and relaxed, sitting in a posture that embodies dignity. It may help to place a small cushion at the small of the back for some support, but make sure that the upper back is self-supporting. Have your hands either palms down on your thighs or palms facing up in your lap, with one hand on top of the other hand and the thumbs touching. See which option feels better for you. If possible, keep the eyes slightly open with a relaxed but stable downward gaze.

What is most important is that you sit in a posture that feels comfortable for your body. Try to feel your way into a posture that is right for you right now, bearing in mind that your body will relax and open the more you practise. To start with you might experience some backache as you train the muscles in your back to sit up straight, rather than hunched over a computer, which is often the default posture in normal life. Therefore, when you start practising, try to sit up straight for a while and then sit back to rest your back, gradually training yourself to sit up straight for longer periods of time. Check on your posture from time to time and correct it if necessary.

It is a myth in Mindfulness meditation that practitioners must sit completely still. If you become uncomfortable in your posture, see if you can feel the discomfort for a while and then decide to move mindfully to ease the discomfort. The mind reflects the body and so if the body moves to a comfortable posture, it supports the mind to be at ease.

We will cover posture sitting on a cushion on the floor later.

Recognising the Unsettled Mind

Set a timer for five minutes and sit comfortably with your back straight, with the intention of doing nothing. If you are used to sitting cross-legged on a cushion you can do that, but it is not necessary. A straight-backed chair is probably best, so you can adapt a posture of alert presence.

Once you are sitting comfortably, simply relax – with your eyes open if possible – and experience being where you are. Feel the pressure of your body resting on the seat and ground; become aware of the space around you; notice how a panoramic visual experience is there and how you naturally become aware of sounds and other sensory stimuli – perhaps a smell of cooking wafts in from next door or maybe a breeze brushes your skin. So this practice is very simple: just allow yourself to be there, experiencing whatever happens when you decide to sit and do nothing.

In a surprisingly short time you will find that you are thinking about something, even though you had decided to do nothing. When you realise you are thinking, simply bring your attention back to being there doing nothing. Once again, before you know it you will have drifted away following some random thought. So once again, when you realise this, bring your attention back to being there doing nothing.

Write down here what you noticed about your experience:

_____

_____

_____

_____

_____

_____

_____

_____

Did you do nothing for the whole five minutes? Or was there some activity going on in your mind? Did you find yourself daydreaming, planning, worrying, remembering, or thinking?

Don't worry if you spent the entire five minutes thinking. This is what we have trained our minds to do throughout our lives. Our education system trains us to be thinking all the time. At work and in daily life we are encouraged to be constantly thinking, to plan our lives and solve our problems. When we are not working the entertainment industry entices us into even more relentless mental activity, through watching television, playing video games, being preoccupied with 24-hour news coverage of many distressing world events, or interacting with our phones. In the modern world little value is placed on resting, doing nothing and being present.

As a result of all this thinking activity we have developed butterfly minds, constantly flitting from one idea to another, preoccupied with thinking all of the time – or maybe a crazy monkey mind, screaming and compulsively jumping from one activity to another. The first step is to recognise that we all have these busy minds – to recognise that there is nothing wrong with this – and to understand that it is possible to begin training our minds in a new habit of being present.

We sat for five minutes in the exercise above with the intention of doing nothing. But, as we have just seen, for most of us the mind was constantly active, producing all kinds of thoughts and feelings. What does that tell us about our mind? It tells us that we are not in control of this very own mind of ours – quite a sobering thought! This is because thoughts arise of their own accord in the mind. It is involuntary, like the heart beating or the process of digesting food. It happens on its own, out of our control. And what is more, we have developed a strong habit of engaging with the thoughts that arise within the mind and thus get caught up in the activity of thinking.

At this point in our training, it is important to recognise that there is a difference between thoughts and thinking. Thoughts naturally arise in our minds. Just as our eyes experience visual objects and our ears experience sounds, so our minds experience thoughts. We would be very worried if we woke up one day and opened our eyes to see nothing, but so many of us expect that Mindfulness meditation will clear our minds of thoughts. This is simply not the case: our minds produce thoughts because that is what they do. Our mind would not be working properly if it wasn't experiencing thoughts, just as our ears would not be working properly if we stopped hearing sounds. So we are not trying to get rid of thoughts in our Mindfulness meditation practice.

Let's say this again and louder:

WE ARE NOT TRYING TO GET RID OF OUR THOUGHTS!

In fact in our Mindfulness practice we are not trying to get rid of anything. Let's go back to the definition of *"knowing what is happening, while it is happening, without preference"*. From this definition we can see that the *"what is happening"* isn't the issue, the issue is *"knowing what is happening"* and accepting what is happening *"without preference"*.

But as we have seen, there is a strong habit to engage with thoughts that naturally arise within the mind and to get involved with these thoughts. This process is driven by preference: what we like, what we do not like or what we experience as neutral. So if nice thoughts and feelings arise we get absorbed in them and try to perpetuate them, but if unpleasant thoughts and feelings arise we try to avoid them and push them away. This is the basic tendency of mind that we are working with in Mindfulness training. The practice is to notice the thoughts and feelings that arise in the mind, and to let them come and go freely with an attitude of acceptance; while at the same time learning to get less and less involved with them. This is the delicate balance that lies at the heart of Mindfulness practice.

The title of this Chapter is *"Start Here and Now"*. It is important to recognise that we start with a butterfly mind or perhaps even a crazy monkey mind. We all start like this. We need to be realistic about it. Furthermore, our compulsive need to engage with thoughts and become involved in thinking is not of our choosing, but is a result of our conditioning from our school, our work and our society. The human mind is tricky and is evolved for survival, not for happiness and tranquillity. This is not of our choosing either. It is very important to acknowledge that we can let ourselves off the hook for having a butterfly or crazy monkey mind and not beat ourselves up about it. Rather, we have the opportunity right now to take responsibility for training our minds to relate differently to the unceasing flow of feelings, sensations and thoughts that move through us.

Our Mindfulness training is about gradually getting to know these minds of ours, without force and without conflict. We are not trying to change anything. Whatever arises in the mind is OK. We are not trying to get rid of thoughts, emotions or sensations. However, we may well find that the changes we desire happen by themselves – if we develop a new habit of regularly practising Mindfulness.

Settling the Mind

Follow the Settling the Mind exercise written out below or follow the guided audio.

Do this exercise for 5 to 10 minutes.

Find a comfortable sitting posture with your back straight and relaxed. If possible, keep your eyes open. Focus in a very relaxed way on your breath. Breathe in a little more deeply than normal and then gently release the breath. Both in-breaths and out-breaths are gentle, so should not be audible. Try to keep in- and out-breaths equal in length, so you may find it useful to count. You may find you breathe in to a count of 3 or 4, in which case your out-breath will be to the same count. So you are now doing two things: regulating your breathing and counting. Despite this, thoughts will continue to pop into your mind, which is totally OK and natural. Don't worry about it. You are not attempting to get rid of thoughts or make your mind go blank. In fact, you are not doing anything besides focusing on breathing and counting. The only difference now is that you do not become involved with the thoughts that pop into your mind. You let them be, without attempting to suppress or become involved with them.

Towards the end of the exercise, you can focus more on the out-breath, imagining that you are releasing involvement with thoughts as you breathe out. Notice that as you release the breath the body relaxes a little. See if the mind can learn from the body – the body releases breath and relaxes, the mind releases involvement with thoughts and begins to settle down.

Do this exercise for about 5 to 10 minutes, then stop the counting and allow your normal breathing rhythm to re-establish itself.

Write down here what you noticed about your experience:

_____

_____

_____

_____

_____

_____

_____

_____

Did your mind settle a bit? Don't worry if it didn't. It takes practice and we will be practising this exercise every day this week.

Sometimes people don't like the counting part of the settling the mind exercise. An alternative way of regulating the breath, so that the in- and out-breath are a similar length, is to say a mantra – a repeated phrase – such as *"I know I breathe in"* on the in-breath and *"I know I breathe out"* on the out-breath.

Sometimes people don't like regulating the breath, so instead you can breathe normally and with each in-breath press down slightly with one of your fingers, starting with the little finger on the left hand and progressing breath by breath through each finger, until you get to the little finger on the right hand. Then start again.

When settling the mind we use a key principle in our training, which is:

ENERGY FOLLOWS FOCUS

When we engage with thoughts and get involved in thinking, we feed energy into this habit and the habit becomes stronger. When we do the settling the mind exercise, we shift our focus to something neutral, namely breathing and counting; and in doing so we withdraw our energy from the process of engaging with thoughts and thinking. Moreover, using the dual focus of regulating the breath and counting during settling provides a strong focus for the mind, which encourages it to settle down. We only do this for a short period of time at the beginning of a period of Mindfulness practice, after we have settled into our posture and reflected on our intention and motivation. When we notice that we have become caught up in thinking during the settling practice, we simply move our focus back to regulating the breathing and counting. This is part of the training in Mindfulness technique.

It is important to have a kind and gentle attitude to our experience as we settle the mind. This is training in our Mindfulness attitude. We know already that we have a butterfly or crazy monkey mind and this habit is not going to change overnight. It is inevitable that our minds will get caught up in thinking, time and time again; and so when we notice we are daydreaming or planning, we take it as an opportunity to exercise the muscle of Mindfulness and come back to regulating the breathing and counting.

Imagine you are training a puppy to sit. Every time it gets up and walks away, you gently bring the puppy back and ask it to sit again, with an encouraging tone of voice. Shouting at the puppy and giving it a hard time would be counterproductive. As with the puppy, so too with the mind: giving ourselves a hard time when our minds wander just makes us more uptight and contracted in our practice.

As we rest our focus on regulating the breath and counting, we simply allow any activity of the mind, such as the arising of thoughts and feelings, to be as it is. Remember, that we are not trying to get rid of thoughts, emotions or sensations, but we are learning to let them be. If we get into a fight with the activity of our mind, our focus is on the struggle and so our energy goes into the struggle and it is unlikely that the mind will settle down!

The mind is naturally inclined to settle if we leave it alone. A jam jar full of muddy water will be dark brown and opaque if we stir up the mud. If we leave the jam jar alone the mud will settle out of the water and the water will become clear. It is the same with the mind. So there is some hope!

To reiterate, it is not the arising of thoughts that disturbs the mind, it is engaging with thoughts and getting carried away into thinking. The practice is to focus our attention on regulating the breathing and counting, and simultaneously to allow thoughts, emotions and sensations to come and go, without interfering with them.

Practice Schedule for the Week after Session One

Each day spend five minutes practising "Recognising the Unsettled Mind". Follow this each day by the Settling the Mind exercise. You can use the guided audio from the MBLC app or on the webpage listed on page 6. Do this each day this week. At the end of the practice, reflect on what happened during your period of practice and make notes below. This is your own personal record.

Day 1

_____

_____

_____

Day 2

_____

_____

_____

Day 3

_____

_____

_____

Day 4

_____

_____

_____

Day 5

_____

_____

_____

Day 6

_____

_____

_____

Day 7

_____

_____

_____

Chapter 3

Session Two – The Body is Always Here and Now

Introducing the Bodyscan Practice

Once we have begun the process of settling the mind the next step is to bring our awareness more fully into the body – a key element of the sitting practice that we will introduce later. This is the bodyscan – an important practice, which deepens the experience of settling and opens us more fully to the inner world of sensation in our bodies. In this practice we move our attention progressively through the body, to notice and feel the sensations that are present in it. It is generally done lying down, but for some people it works better to sit on a chair or cushion.

Perhaps you can try this out right now and bring your attention to your feet noticing any physical sensations that are present within this part of the body. You may notice sensations of contact between your feet and the ground; perhaps sensations of temperature or pressure. A variety of sensations is possible – or you may feel no sensations in the feet just now, and that is fine too. Also, notice the difference between thinking about the feet and directly feeling them. The bodyscan practice is about directly feeling the sensations in the body and is not about thinking about or imagining the body.

So the practice is simple: just feel whatever sensations are present in the feet, not trying to change anything, but just allowing the sensations to be as they are.

Let's explore the bodyscan practice in terms of our working definition of Mindfulness:

Knowing what is happening, while it is happening, without preference.

We practise the Mindfulness technique of *"knowing what is happening, while it is happening"* by noticing any physical sensations present in the part of the body we are attending to. When we notice that we are caught up in thinking, we gently guide our focus back to feeling the sensations in the same part of the body. It is likely that our mind will drift off into thinking many times. Each time we notice this and bring our attention back to the bodyscan, we are strengthening our *'muscle of Mindfulness'*. In this way the bodyscan builds our capacity for paying attention. We train to move our attention around different parts of the body, sometimes with a narrow focus, for example on the big toe, and sometimes with a wide focus, for example on the whole body.

We practise the Mindfulness attitude of *'without preference'* by being open and accepting of whatever happens during our bodyscan practice, whether pleasant, unpleasant or neutral. We simply notice whatever sensations are present – strong sensations, no sensations and the whole range of sensations in between these extremes – and allowing them to be just as they are. We train to welcome sensations to be here on their own terms, even painful ones, with an attitude of *'nothing is wrong'*. We practise not interfering with, fixing or trying to get rid of unwanted sensations.

It is important to recognise that the body is always here and now. The mind tends to be all over the place, in London, Mars or even Middle Earth! It also tends to be all over time, in the close or distant past or imagined future. The body is always where we are now and it is always in the present. For this reason it is a great ally in our Mindfulness practice and in our daily lives. Thus, the bodyscan practice puts us in touch with the here and now.

The bodyscan also puts us in touch with this living, breathing, feeling body of ours. Many of us in modern society live completely in our heads and out of touch with the body; cut off from the neck downwards. This body of ours does so much for us: it breathes, it digests, it pumps blood, it enables us to move around and interact with our environments, and it supports the mind. Most of the time we take all of this for granted, and so the bodyscan is an opportunity to get to know our body in a gentle, kindly way and even express some gratitude towards it. It is also an opportunity to practise 'beginner's mind': exploring this body of ours with a fresh and curious quality of awareness, as if we are getting to know it for the first time.

The body also feels emotions: being in touch with our body allows us to get in touch with our emotions. We can get to know what anger feels like, perhaps a tightening in the shoulders or jaw; or what anxiety feels like, perhaps butterflies in the tummy or a racing heart. When we are attuned to how the body feels, we can begin to recognise how it changes as we experience different emotions. This can help us in daily life to recognise when we are experiencing an emotional reaction to the circumstances around us. This can be a signal to become present, take a few Mindful breaths and to respond mindfully, instead of reacting automatically. For example, we may receive an email which makes us angry. The bodyscan practice teaches us to connect with the angry feeling in our body; to stay present with the sensations and hold off replying until we have had a chance to calm down, rather than firing off an angry reply, which might then just inflame the situation.

Many of us do not like our bodies. We think they are too big or too small, too ugly, too weak, or defective in some way. This can mean that our relationship with our body can be complex and dysfunctional. The bodyscan gradually builds a more healthy relationship with our bodies. It helps us experience our body 'from the inside' and we learn to open up to and accept its full range of feelings, energies and sensations. In this way we begin to appreciate an underlying wholeness that does not depend on how our bodies appear from the outside. This is the basis of genuine gratitude and well-being. During the bodyscan we are also able to observe many of our habitual patterns of thought and behaviour and get to know them better. For example, we may notice that we want to become absorbed in pleasant sensations and avoid unpleasant sensations. We may notice that we want to do the practice perfectly and that we get angry with ourselves when we get drowsy or fall asleep. We may notice that we want to rush through the practice, and experience boredom or frustration that it is lasting so long.

This is all very useful learning, because we are becoming more familiar with the habit patterns that play out in our lives. The body is a touchstone that alerts us to a variety of triggers that spark off unconscious reactions and drives. Through paying attention to the body we have an anchor in the present moment and a source of wisdom to get to know ourselves better. All of this arises from the seemingly simple practice of the bodyscan. Now let's do the practice and begin this process of learning for ourselves.

Bodyscan Practice

Follow the Bodyscan exercise written out below or follow the guided audio.

Do this exercise for about 30 minutes.

Find a comfortable place to lie down, on the bed or on the floor, remembering that your intention is to foster awareness and wakefulness. If you do fall asleep then become aware of the process of moving into and out of sleep and don't give yourself a hard time. Make sure that you will be warm enough and cover yourself with a blanket if necessary. If you are uncomfortable lying down you can choose an alternative position, such as lying on your side or sitting. It is OK to move if you need to.

Close your eyes and focus for a while on the rising and falling of the breath in the body. This breath renews life with every in-breath. It lets go of what is no longer needed with each out-breath. Notice the sense of letting go as each out-breath exits the body. Feel the flowing of the entire breath throughout the body. Take a few minutes to have a sense of the body as a whole, from head to toe, from the left side to the right side, the outline of your skin, and the weight of the body on the ground. Notice the points where the body is in contact with the surfaces it rests upon.

Throughout this practice, whenever you notice that the mind has wandered, and is caught up in thinking, simply notice where it has wandered to and gently bring your attention back to feeling the sensations in the body.

Now bring your focus to the big toes on both of the feet and explore the sensations that you find here. You are not trying to make anything happen – just feeling what you are feeling. There is no right or wrong way to feel. There may be strong sensations, no sensations or something in between. Gradually broaden your focus to include the other toes, the soles of the feet and the other parts of the feet. Imagine as you breathe in that your breath is flowing down to the feet, and as you breathe out that the breath is flowing out of the feet into the space surrounding the feet, allowing the feet to be held in awareness. On the next out-breath, let go of the feet.

Then move your focus to the ankles and notice whatever sensations are there. Then gradually move on to feel the calves, then the knees and thighs, simply noticing whatever sensations are there and allowing them to be as they are. Once again imagine as you breathe in that your breath is flowing down the legs, and as you breathe out that the breath is flowing out of the legs into the space surrounding the legs, allowing your legs to be held in awareness. On the next out-breath, let go of the legs.

If you experience strong or unpleasant experiences, such as pain or agitation, simply notice the patterns of physical sensation that the mind labels as pain or agitation. As you breathe in imagine that the breath touches the area of strong sensation and as you breathe out imagine that the breath spreads out from the area of strong sensation,

with a sense of softening around the strong sensation. Do this as a way
of welcoming the strong sensation as one part of your experience in this
moment, not as a way to fix or get rid of the sensation. After a while, if
you need to, you can move mindfully to ease any physical discomfort.
Only stay with a difficult sensation for a few moments and then return
to the bodyscan practice, wherever you are up to in the body.

Next move your focus to the buttocks and notice whatever sensations
are there. Perhaps you feel sensations of contact with whatever the
buttocks are resting upon. Now gradually in stages, allow your focus
to move to the pelvic region, the belly, the lower back, the upper back,
the ribcage, the heart and lungs and the shoulders. Simply feel any
sensations that appear as you focus on the different body parts. Now
broaden your focus to become aware of the whole torso, from the hips
to the shoulders. Feel the motion of the breath through the torso. Now
imagine as you breathe in that your breath is flowing down into the
torso, and as you breathe out that the breath is flowing out of the
torso into the space surrounding it, allowing the torso to be held in
awareness. On the next out-breath, let go of the torso.

Next bring your focus to the fingertips, then to the fingers and
hands. Notice any sensation in the palms of the hands. Notice what
the hands feel like at rest. Then gradually move your attention up the
lower arms, noticing the sensations in the elbows, upper arms and
then the shoulders. Now imagine as you breathe in that your breath is
flowing down into the arms and hands, and as you breathe out that the
breath is flowing out of the arms and hands into the space surrounding
them, allowing the arms and hands to be held in awareness. On the
next out-breath, let go of the arms and hands.

Now gradually bring your awareness to the neck, the jaw, the
face and the scalp. Notice any tension held in the muscles around the
forehead, around the eyes, the jaw and the mouth. Allow any feelings
in the head and neck region to be just as they are, softening around
them with your awareness. Now imagine as you breathe in that your
breath is flowing into the head and neck region, and as you breathe
out that the breath is flowing out of the head and neck region into the

space surrounding it, allowing your head and neck region to be held in awareness. On the next out-breath, let go of the head and neck region.

And now, bring your awareness back to the breathing and notice any feeling of effort as you breathe in, and any softening as you breathe out. Allow your experience to be just as it is – nothing wrong. Now imagine as you breathe in that your breath is flowing down into the centre of the body, and as you breathe out that the breath is flowing from the centre of the body into the space surrounding the body, allowing the whole body to be held in awareness. On the next out-breath, let go of the whole body.

Become aware of the quality of your experience and note any emotional tones present without judging them. When you are ending your practice, start by slowly moving the body, perhaps wiggling your toes and fingers, taking time and making sure not to move out of the practice too quickly.

Write down here what you noticed about your experience during this practice:

_____

_____

_____

_____

_____

_____

_____

When some people start doing the bodyscan they feel very little in their bodies, but over time and with practice gradually more and more subtle sensations reveal themselves. With practice the connection between the mind and body becomes stronger.

When others start doing the bodyscan they fall asleep, often within a few minutes. This is absolutely fine. There is no need to beat yourself up about it, as this is simply reinforcing an unhelpful habit. Instead put your energy into setting an intention of 'falling awake', without making this intention into an expectation. If you become drowsy, open your eyes and take the opportunity to practise becoming aware of the drowsy mind that moves towards and then back out of sleep.

Some people experience restlessness, twitching and restless leg syndrome. This is an opportunity to practise being in touch with difficult sensations and to practise breathing into and out of difficult sensations. It is also an opportunity to practise allowing your experience to be just as it is. However, if the sensations become too troublesome you can practise kindness and move mindfully to another position, for example sitting or mindfully walking.

If you do not connect with the bodyscan practice, that is fine too. You can instead practise mindful walking or mindful movement as a way of building the connection between your mind and body. Do try, however, to come back to the bodyscan practice later in your training, once you have done more Mindfulness practice, and see if anything has changed. Be playful and curious!

Mindfulness in Daily Life

One aim of this course is to develop a regular Mindfulness practice that we do each day. We can refer to this as our formal practice. However, it is just as important to practise Mindfulness in daily life, as this is where we will see most of the benefits from our formal practice, especially in the beginning. In fact, we could see our formal practice as 'practising to practise' with the heart of the practice being how we live our lives.

Again, it may be useful to go back to our working definition of Mindfulness: *"knowing what is happening while it is happening, without preference"*; but this time we are knowing what is happening as we go about our daily lives, with an attitude of gently making space for the ups and downs of our inner experience. It might be useful to point out at this stage that *"without preference"* in this context does not mean that we just put up with anything that happens in our daily lives and just allow it. For example, it does not mean that if someone insults us at work we just roll over and allow this to happen. *"Without preference"* refers to a non-judgmental attitude to the inner flow of experience in the mind. In this example it means that we are aware of and make space for what arises inwardly, like indignation, hurt and anger. We still take action to redress what happens externally, but in a way that is wise and constructive.

To help us cultivate Mindfulness in daily life we begin by choosing particular activities and set an intention to do them mindfully each day. Then over time we might notice that we naturally become mindful at times during our daily life. We start with one activity per day and then add another new activity every week. It is best to choose short activities to start with, such as eating a piece of fruit, rather than eating a full meal, as it may be difficult to be mindful during a whole meal.

Here are some activities you could choose:

- Mindfully eating a snack
- Mindfully brushing your teeth
- Mindfully stacking the dishwasher or doing the washing up
- Mindfully showering
- Mindfully making a cup of tea or coffee
- Mindfully picking up the phone

- Mindfully walking from the house to the car, bus stop or station
- Mindfully peeling the potatoes
- Mindfully going up the stairs
- Mindfully switching on the computer and waiting for it to load

When we do our mindful daily life activity we can focus on different aspects of our experience as we do the activity, such as the feeling of our feet on the floor, physical sensations in the body, body movements, sights, sounds, smells and tastes.

The main problem with Mindfulness in daily life is remembering to be mindful! Recall that the word in the Pali language for Mindfulness, *'sati'*, has the meaning of recollectedness or remembrance. We might set our intention to walk up and down the stairs mindfully and then get to the end of the day and realise that every time we walked up and down the stairs we were caught up in thinking and operating on autopilot, completely out of touch with our experience. As always, there is no point in beating ourselves up about this, as this just reinforces an unhelpful habit. Instead we can use a Mindfulness trigger. For example, we might tie a brightly coloured head scarf or tie to the bannister to remind ourselves to be mindful when climbing the stairs. We can also place markers, like stickers or notes, in strategic locations to remind us of our intention to be mindful. Furthermore, we can use our phones and computers to aid the process of recollection and set Mindfulness alarms that remind us to be present, even if it is just for three mindful breaths.

Choosing a mindful activity in daily life is part of the home practice this week.

Write down here your daily life activity:

_____

_____

_____

Write down here how you are going to remember to do your daily life activity:

_____

_____

_____

Introducing Kindness

Be kind to everyone, and if you can't be kind then at least do no harm.
HH Dalai Lama

When it comes to our Mindfulness definition, training in kindness is part of the *"without preference"* part of the definition. It is part of our training in attitude.

When we practise Mindfulness, we get to know ourselves better; and in particular we get to know more about our habitual patterns of thought and behaviour. It is a bit like turning a dimmer switch up in a room. In a similar way Mindfulness increases our inner awareness and this starts to reveal more and more of what is in the room of our mind. Some of the things we get to know about ourselves we won't like, perhaps that we are more selfish, angry or anxious than we had previously realised. Usually, when we see something about ourselves that we don't like, we give ourselves a hard time. This is counterproductive, because it merely strengthens the voice of our self-critic, whereas it might be more skilful to cultivate a kind and encouraging voice in the face of our difficulties. It is like the example of the two kinds of teacher (or puppy trainer!) – one who shouts when we make mistakes or one who encourages us when we fall short of our goals. Which teacher would you prefer?

Let's now explore kindness in a very simple and pragmatic way. Think back over the last week or so and recall some of the acts of kindness that someone else did for you. They don't have to be big acts of kindness, like donating a kidney! They can be small acts of kindness, like someone making a cup of tea or a meal for you, someone holding a door open for you, or someone making way for you in a queue of traffic.

Write here some acts of kindness you have experienced from others in the last week or so:

_____

_____

_____

_____

_____

_____

Now think about some acts of kindness you did for others over the last week or so. Again they don't have to be major acts of kindness; they can be everyday acts of kindness, such as sending someone a kind text, saying something to cheer someone up or carrying someone's bag.

Write here some acts of kindness you have done for others in the last week or so:

_____

_____

_____

Sometimes people find it more difficult to remember acts of kindness they did for others in comparison to acts of kindness they received. It is as if we are a bit embarrassed to acknowledge our good points, such as our acts of kindness. Is this the case for you?

Finally, think about some acts of kindness you did for yourself over the last week or so. Perhaps you made yourself a cup of tea after a busy day, ran yourself a hot bath or took some time out of your busy schedule to practise some Mindfulness!

Write here some acts of kindness you have done for yourself in the last week or so:

_____

_____

_____

Sometimes people find that they can more easily be kind to others than to themselves. Is this the case for you?

Now we have reflected on some examples of kindness from our own experience, let's look at a definition:

Kindness is a genuine wish for the happiness and well-being of ourselves and others.

People often think that kindness is a form of indulgence, but if what we are doing is motivated by the wish for the happiness and well-being of ourselves or others, then how can this be indulgent? We can check the difference between kindness and indulgence by examining our motivation. For example, is it kind or indulgent to have a third glass of wine, or a second piece of cake after a stressful day? In the short term we might feel better, but having that extra glass of wine or slice of cake is probably reinforcing an unskilful habit of coping with stress and is unlikely to be in the interest of our long-term happiness and well-being.

At this point it may be useful to reflect that our bodies and minds have evolved to survive and procreate, not necessarily to be happy. Those ancestors of ours who ran up a tree when they heard a rustle in the grass were the ones that survived and were not eaten by predators, and they were the ones who passed on their genes to us. In this way we have evolved to be very sensitive to threats. Unfortunately this tendency is reinforced in today's society where we are surrounded by threatening messages from news coverage of terrible crimes, wars and natural disasters, and from the advertising industry telling us we are not good enough until we get the right car, house, body shape, and so on.

These messages can cause us to imagine many threatening situations that may never happen, but the brain nonetheless still experiences them as threats. As Rick Hanson pointed out in his book *Buddha's Brain: The Practical Neuroscience of Happiness, Love, and Wisdom* (2009), threat sticks in the mind like Velcro and kindness slides off the mind like a silk scarf. For this reason it is wise to counteract our default threat tendency by consciously training our minds to notice and appreciate acts of kindness.

To illustrate the link between what we imagine and how we

feel, consider what would happen if we only focused on instances when other people were *un*kind to us. We would clearly not end up feeling very good. But the strange thing is that we often tend to dwell on memories of other people being unkind or saying unpleasant things to us. Evolutionary Psychologist Professor Paul Gilbert loves to use the example of going to a shopping complex where nine shopkeepers are very polite and helpful, and one is rude and offhand. Who do you talk about when you go home? Invariably we tend to gloss over the people who were kind and focus on the one who was not. It is helpful to remember that we are not to blame for this; it is just how our brain has evolved. But it is also important to bear in mind that if we continually stimulate our threat system, this has the effect of blocking helpful memories and positive brain patterns. The question we need to ask ourselves is: where do we want to shine the spotlight of our attention?

This brings us back to one of the core principles in our training: *'energy follows focus'*. This means that our energies flow in the direction of what we focus on, so if we feed positive thoughts and feelings we feel happy, while if we feed negative thoughts and feelings we feel miserable. Similarly, if we dwell on unpleasant events in the past or continually worry about possible threats in the future, we then reinforce the threat setting in our brain, and end up feeling more and more stressed and anxious. However, if we pay more attention to thinking and acting in kind ways we reinforce this habit in our minds, and research shows that it results in greater happiness and well-being.

We begin this process by setting our intention to practise kindness in our formal Mindfulness practice and in our daily lives. Then we clarify our motivation by reflecting on why it would be helpful to experience more kindness in our lives, and how this might benefit both ourselves and those around us. We can then do the kindness exercise below on a regular basis and practise recognising kindness when it happens in our lives –

really allowing ourselves to bathe in the feeling of kindness. We can practise random acts of kindness by taking opportunities that occur in our daily lives to be kind. We can practise walking around town smiling at the people we pass and in our heads wishing them to be happy. Kindness is catchy and so if we smile at someone with a genuine wish for them to be happy, then they are more likely to smile at the next person they pass in the street.

Just as it is important to practise kindness, so too is it important to notice when we are closing down to kindness. Many of us feel resistance to giving or receiving kindness, and we can instead experience feelings such as anger, sadness or anxiety. This is perfectly normal and it is an opportunity to welcome and get to know our blocks to kindness. We don't need to fix these blocks and resistances, nor do we need to contrive feelings of kindness when they do not naturally flow. It is enough just to be aware of these blocks and hold them with an attitude of acceptance. This in itself is an act of kindness. It also creates the conditions for these blocks to soften and for the energy of kindness to gradually flow around them. Some of us may even find ourselves crying when we do the kindness exercise. This is absolutely fine and it is a sign that the energy of kindness is beginning to flow.

Memories of Kindness Exercise

Follow the Memories of Kindness exercise written out below or follow the guided audio.

Do this exercise for about 15 minutes.

Sit in a relaxed and dignified posture and begin by bringing to mind your intention for the practice, for example to explore the experience of kindness. Then spend a minute or so reflecting on your motivation – why you want to cultivate a kinder atmosphere within your mind. How might this benefit you and those around you?

Then settle your mind as we have done before. Now bring to mind a memory of when someone was kind to you. Recall the detail of what happened and go through it in your mind. Remember how you felt when this person was kind to you. As you bring to mind the memory allow your experience to unfold in its own way, simply noticing what happens and remembering that there is no right or wrong way to feel. Do you notice any thoughts about the memory? How does this act of kindness feel in your body now? Allow yourself to experience whatever feelings are present for a couple of minutes, becoming familiar with any felt sense of kindness or any felt sense of resistance.

Now bring to mind a memory of when you were kind to someone else. It may take some time for a memory to emerge. Recall the detail of what happened and go through it in your mind. Recall how you felt when you were kind to this person. Do you notice any thoughts about the memory? How does this act of kindness feel in your body now? Allow yourself to feel any sense of kindness or resistance as you recall this memory.

Finally, bring to mind a memory of when you were kind to yourself. Recall the detail of what happened and go through it in your mind. Remember how you felt and notice any thoughts about the memory. How does this act of kindness feel in your body now? Allow yourself to experience whatever feelings are present for a couple of minutes, becoming familiar with any felt sense of kindness or any felt sense of resistance.

To end the practice let go of the memories, feel the weight of your body resting on the ground and your breath moving through the body. Notice any leftover feelings from the practice and gently soften around how they feel in the body.

Write down here what you noticed about your experience:

_____

_____

_____

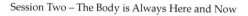

You may notice that bringing these memories to mind creates warm feelings of kindness inside of you, even if they are just faint glimmers.

In your daily life see if you can notice acts of kindness that are done for you or that you do for others, however small they may be. Tune in to how these acts of kindness feel in your body. Take time to bathe your mind and body in kindness whenever the opportunity presents itself.

Once you become familiar with this felt sense of kindness, see whether you can bring this to your Mindfulness practice and to your daily life so that you practise and live with an attitude of open and kindly curiosity towards whatever arises in your experience.

Practice Schedule for the Week after Session Two

Formal Practice

Alternate doing the bodyscan practice with the memories of kindness exercise. You can use the guided audio from the MBLC app or on the webpage listed on page 6. At the end of the period of practice, reflect on what happened during it and make notes below. In particular, notice any particular body sensations you noticed during the practice. Do this each day this week. This is your own personal record.

Day 1

_____

_____

_____

Day 2

_____

_____

_____

Day 3

_____

_____

_____

Day 4

_____

_____

_____

Day 5

_____

_____

_____

Day 6

_____

_____

_____

Day 7

_____

_____

_____

Informal Daily Life Practice

Do the Mindfulness in Daily Life activity that you wrote down above at least once each day and find opportunities to do random acts of kindness. Then at least once in the week, when you are walking around town, smile at the people you see and wish them to be happy in your mind. Describe below what you noticed.

Day 1

_____

_____

_____

Day 2

_____

_____

_____

Day 3

_____

_____

_____

Day 4

_____

_____

_____

Day 5

_____

_____

_____

Day 6

_____

_____

_____

Day 7

_____

_____

_____

Chapter 4

Session Three – Introducing Mindfulness Support

Review of Practice

Practising Mindfulness can be compared to running a marathon. If we were planning to run it in 10 weeks' time, we would not spend our time reading about marathons as preparation. We would follow a training program that involved running regularly and gradually increasing the distance so that our bodies became fit and ready to run the marathon. It is the same with Mindfulness. If we want to become more mindful in our lives then reading about it simply is not enough – we need to practise. The research evidence shows that those who do formal Mindfulness practice at least 6 days a week benefit most from a Mindfulness course. By 'formal practice' we mean devoting a time and space to practising Mindfulness in a systematic and structured way. There is less benefit for those who only do informal, daily life practice.

It can be difficult to develop a new habit of daily Mindfulness practice. It can also be difficult to find the time to devote 20 to 30 minutes a day for Mindfulness practice.

Nonetheless, Jon Kabat-Zinn says:

Practise as if your life depends on it – and it probably does.

Moreover, Rob Nairn says:

Mindfulness practice is the most important thing we can do in our lives.

These views might seem a bit extreme, but the authors of this book have worked with many people whose lives have been transformed by Mindfulness practice. What we notice is that it is always those people who commit to a daily formal practice that benefit the most.

So what can help us in developing a daily formal practice?

If our lifestyle allows it, it is best to practise at the same time each day. For many people, getting up 30 minutes earlier than usual and practising first thing in the morning is best. Others prefer to practise in the evening, while there are some who find it best to practise when they finish work. It is important for each of us to find out what best suits our personality and lifestyle.

It can also be helpful to practise in the same place each day – like in a corner of our bedroom or study. This then becomes our safe space for practice. We can even decorate this space so that it becomes our very own sacred space. The mind works by association, and so sitting in the same place each day that is specially designated for practice can allow the mind to settle more easily.

We can also be creative in finding time and space during the day to do formal practice. This might be on our commute to work. If we are on a train or a bus we can put some headphones on and practise while listening to guided instructions. If we are driving to work we can drive in silence, and use the act of driving as a Mindfulness support, while staying present and attentive to distracting thoughts. If we have to walk somewhere regularly, we can make this our Mindfulness practice; or if we do regular exercise, such as running, swimming or gardening, we can make this a mindful movement practice.

What really doesn't help, however, is giving ourselves a hard time if we don't practice. This turns Mindfulness into yet another thing we beat ourselves up for, and very soon it can be seen as a negative experience. To remedy this, we can acknowledge that it is difficult to develop this new habit. It takes patience and persistent practice and requires supportive conditions. What is crucial, however, is the wish to practise – recognising how important it is and forming the intention to make Mindfulness a cornerstone of our life. Everything else follows from this.

This is why the Mindfulness Association runs a series of four-weekend trainings over a period of nine months. It needs that amount of time for Mindfulness to become a living experience, and it needs a structured path of teaching and group support for it to bear fruit. In our experience it generally takes until weekend four for course participants to develop the habit of practising regularly. So we can let ourselves off the hook if we don't settle into a regular daily practice right away.

But that isn't the end of the matter. If we did not practise today, at the end of the day we can openly acknowledge this – without shame – and reflect on some of the reasons why, such as lack of time, feeling tired, or wanting to watch television. In this way we are learning directly from our experience, which is an important part of Mindfulness training. We can then reaffirm our intention to practise the following day. Next, we can reflect on our motivation: all the reasons why *we* want to practise Mindfulness. List at least five reasons. Then as soon as we wake up the next morning we can bring to mind our intention to practise and these five reasons why *we* want to practise.

In this way we are skilfully working with the principle of 'Energy follows focus'. We don't put energy into beating ourselves up for not practising, because this merely reinforces a destructive habit that results in more self-criticism and shame. Instead we focus on our intention and motivation and so put energy into the wellspring from which the practice of Mindfulness flows. In so doing, the habit of practising Mindfulness will grow and grow until one day we may well find that it has become effortless. Bear in mind that this may take several years! At a very pragmatic level, however, it is better to practise 10 or 15 minutes a day than 30 minutes once or twice a week because then we have something to build on, perhaps by adding an extra 5 minutes every month or so.

Settling, Grounding, Resting and Mindfulness Support

We will focus now on the routine for our Mindfulness sitting practice, which has the following components:

- Posture
- Intention & Motivation
- Settling
- Grounding
- Resting
- Support
- Sharing

This sequence might seem complicated to start with, but once we are familiar with the different stages, they flow naturally from one into the next. These stages are helpful for beginners so that they have very clear, step-by-step instructions for practising Mindfulness. It is a bit like learning to drive a car. In the beginning it is useful to have very clear instructions on how to turn on the ignition, release the hand brake, use the clutch and gears, and so on. Then once we are familiar with the stages we no longer need to think about them; we just get in the car and drive. Practising Mindfulness is similar.

We have already looked at the posture for sitting on a chair, and later in this chapter we will look at the posture for sitting on a cushion on the floor. Posture is very important, because it is a way of placing our body in readiness for practice. We have also looked at intention and motivation, which is a way of placing our minds in readiness for practice. The two are closely connected, because once the body is in place, it holds the attitude of mind required for practice. We then practised settling the mind as a way of calming down the activity and agitation in it. Without doing this stage it might be hard to even begin practising. It is like steadying a horse and placing a saddle on it before we climb on to ride it. As we mentioned before, we usually do this for a few minutes at the beginning of our practice session.

Now we will look at grounding, resting and the Mindfulness support of sound. We will look at the Mindfulness support of breath in the next chapter. We end our practice session with a sharing, so as to acknowledge the benefit we get from our Mindfulness practice and our wish to share it with others.

Grounding

Once we have settled the mind, we move on to grounding in the body. In fact, settling naturally leads into grounding. Through paying attention to the out-breath in the settling stage, our centre of gravity drops from the head into the body and we feel the weight of our body on the ground. When we guide the grounding stage, we often use the following phrase: "mind resting in the body like the body resting on the ground". These words signal to us that we are switching from the sympathetic nervous system, which draws us up into our heads, to the parasympathetic system, which connects us more fully with our bodies. This movement into embodiment is crucial for Mindfulness because the body is an anchor that is always here and now, whereas the mind flits all over the place. Moreover, being grounded in the body slows us down and broadens our field of awareness, which are key elements of Mindfulness – as opposed to being on full throttle, locked in our heads and tightly focused on what we want or do not want.

Now once we feel some connection to our bodies and to the ground we are sitting on, we then become aware of how we are feeling in the body. We might feel pain in our shoulders, a knot of tension in our stomach or heaviness in the abdomen, or a variety of other sensations. In life we often try to avoid uncomfortable sensations like these by moving away; but with grounding we practise approaching these sensations with an attitude of softening and allowing. This has two important effects: firstly feeling sensations in the body holds our mind present and is a strong anchor for our Mindfulness practice; and secondly the attitude of allowing counteracts our tendency to react to our experience by grasping at it or trying to push it away. Often when people are asked what the main effect of Mindfulness is in their lives, they tend to remark that they are more accepting and less reactive towards their thoughts, feelings and sensations. Grounding is a key element in this process.

There are various ways of approaching grounding. One option is to scan our attention down the body, a bit like a short bodyscan, noticing body sensations and allowing them to be as they are. Another option is to notice particular parts of the body, such as the hands resting on the knees or in the lap, the buttocks resting on the chair or cushion, or the feet resting on the ground. Yet another option is to let our attention be drawn to whatever sensations are predominant, and simply feeling them and accepting them. We can deepen this process by softening around strong sensations as we breathe out, as a way of welcoming these sensations into our experience.

Through grounding we get a sense of how the ground unconditionally supports the body. This helps us to allow our experience to be as it is and there is growing awareness that the body will hold our experience of mind just like the ground holds our body. We can ease up holding on so tightly to our inner dramas of thought and feeling, and begin to let go. In so doing, we get a glimpse of inner space, and we can begin to relax into this space. Once again the body helps us here. When we let go of the body and allow it to be held by the ground, we then become aware of the space around the body: the body exists in space and is surrounded by it. This naturally leads into the next stage, which is resting.

Resting

This brings us to the heart of our approach to Mindfulness practice. Many people puzzle over the term 'resting'. But it simply means being with what is present in our experience now. Mindfulness is not about finding some exalted state of bliss, peace or freedom from thought. It is more like coming home at the end of the day and dropping ourselves down on our favourite armchair. For many of us 'resting' might involve mulling over thoughts of the day while we sit on this armchair, but true resting is feeling the weight of our body on the armchair and letting all the thoughts and feelings just be there, while opening our senses to all that we see, feel, hear and sense – making space for all of this. All the most profound techniques of meditation just come down to this. It is simple but not easy.

As we can see, a key element of resting is 'being with' our experience as it is. This implies being aware of what is going on, allowing ourselves to feel what is going on, and not resisting what is going on. Now this brings us to the heart of what Mindfulness is. It brings together the method and attitude that are part of our working definition of Mindfulness: *"knowing what is happening while it is happening without preference."* It requires us to be fully present and accepting. From this we can see that 'resting' or 'being with', simple as they sound, actually contain the full depth and range of Mindfulness practice. Ironically, there is a lot going on with resting even though it comes down to doing nothing!

In this way, being with our experience as it unfolds, we begin to sense space around our experience. We begin to recognise this space and rest in it. This is not an empty space but the space of awareness. It is like a light that illuminates everything it shines on. So through Mindfulness practice we come to feel and taste this awareness, and it becomes our lifelong friend. Mindfulness is the method that brings us home to awareness. Even though we might be feeling anxious or tense or sad, awareness is always there, witnessing this; but awareness is never anxious or tense or sad. So at its deepest level 'resting' means resting in the awareness that permeates every aspect of our waking lives. Perhaps this is a bit advanced, but it is useful to know where this path goes, so that there is a sense of vision and purpose to our practice.

In the words of a great Tibetan master, Gendun Rinpoche:

> ... Wanting to gasp the ungraspable, you exhaust yourself in vain.
> As soon as you relax this grasping, space is there,
> open, inviting and comfortable.
> So, make use of it. All is yours already.
> Don't search any further.
> Don't go into the inextricable jungle looking for the elephant who is already quietly at home.
> Nothing to do, nothing to force, nothing to want
> And everything happens by itself.

In practice, once we have gone through the stage of grounding, we *find ourselves* resting. So there is nothing more to do. It is simple really: we show up where we are in the body, we open up to how we feel, and then we just rest there. In the words of Gendun Rinpoche: "nothing to do, nowhere to go, nothing to achieve, and everything happens by itself."

One way of getting a feel for this quality of resting is paying attention to the moments before we fall asleep. We all rest our minds just before we fall asleep. Therefore, it can be useful to practise Mindfulness as we fall asleep to get to know the quality of the resting mind. The bodyscan can also help us, if we are one of those people who generally fall asleep in a bodyscan. We can become curious about how the mind feels in the drowsy state before we fall asleep. The idea of resting the mind in our sitting practice is to *'fall awake'* and simply be aware of our experience:

knowing what is happening while it is happening, without doing anything.

Of course, when we rest our mind in this way it is not very long before it gets caught up in thinking, so this is when we introduce our Mindfulness support.

Mindfulness Support

It is important to be realistic about Mindfulness practice. Our minds are strongly conditioned to be distracted, and furthermore they have evolved to be this way. So we can let ourselves off the hook if we get frustrated by our perpetually wandering mind. We did not design our brain and it is not our fault that it operates the way it does. In fact, there is part of the brain called the 'Default Mode Network' that is designed to keep us constantly on the alert for threats and things we need to acquire to survive. So in the beginning it is unlikely for us to be able to rest in a state of spacious awareness for very long. What is more likely is that we will touch briefly on the experience of resting and then very quickly our mind will flit off into thinking, planning or dreaming. This is normal and nothing is wrong. This is important because beginners may think they are failing if their mind gets distracted. In fact, seeing more and more clearly how we get distracted is a positive sign – it is a sign of a growing awareness. This might feel uncomfortable but at least we are seeing what is going on, rather than living our lives distracted and unaware.

But we can gradually work with the process of distraction. This is the role of a Mindfulness support. It is a neutral focus in the present moment that provides our attention with something to return to when we get lost in thinking. It is useful to have something to come back to so as to anchor us in the present, just like an anchor holds a boat in place. The anchor will hold the boat in place notwithstanding how bad the weather is, and similarly our Mindfulness support helps us stay present even if the mind becomes stormy and restless.

So far in this course we have used body sensations as a Mindfulness support in the bodyscan, mindful movement and grounding. We used regulating the breath and counting as a Mindfulness support when we practised settling the mind. So we already have some familiarity in working with a support. We will now explore it in more detail, and then look at using sound and breathing as Mindfulness supports.

When we use a Mindfulness support we don't focus on it to the exclusion of everything else. This is a common mistake in the beginning. People can hold on to the support for dear life and unwittingly ward off thoughts, with the underlying belief that concentrating on the support is a sign of meditation going well, whilst becoming involved in thinking is a sign of things going wrong. This is not helpful because it results in suppression, and our minds can become very tight and contracted. What is important is to maintain a light and steady focus on the support whilst also being aware of any activity going on within the mind and around us.

A useful analogy is that of a cocktail waiter walking through a crowd of people holding a tray of glasses filled to the brim with the finest champagne. The waiter needs to keep his eye on the tray of glasses, but he also needs to be aware of the people moving around him. If he only focuses on the tray of glasses he will in all likelihood bump into people around him, and so spill the champagne. On the other hand, if he just pays attention to the people around him and does not keep his eye on the tray, the glasses are likely to spill too. So he needs to keep his eye on *both*, focused mainly on the champagne glasses, but also aware of all the activity around him. This is the quality of attention required in using a Mindfulness support.

Something else to remember in using a support is not to lose track of the previous stages of our practice routine. We do not work through the routine like a tick list leaving the previous stages behind as we move on to the next stage: first posture, then intention and motivation, then settling, and so on. We *build on* the previous stages and they remain part of our practice when we come to the stage of using a support. The posture remains in place, and it holds the intention and motivation. We indeed do let go of the settling phase, but it leads into grounding and resting, which become the basis for the stage of using a Mindfulness support.

This is very important because our practice rests on a foundation that is made of different levels. When it comes to the support, for example sound, our attention rests on it lightly, but we maintain awareness of our bodies resting on the ground; awareness of the space around ourselves; and activity happening in that space. As a rule of thumb, we could say that 80% of our attention remains with grounding and resting, and 20% of our attention rests on the support. When we lose awareness and get lost in thought, our intention alerts us to this fact (we remember that we sat down to be mindful) and reminds us gently to bring our attention back to the support. This in turn brings us back to where we are: mind resting in body, body resting on the ground. So we come back to all of our experience, not just to the support itself.

People sometimes wonder how you can be aware of a Mindfulness support, whilst also being aware of your body and the activity going on around. So let's explore this using a simple example. As you read this page, feel your feet on the ground. Wiggling your toes can help to get a sense of the feet. Feel any sensations of contact between your feet and the ground beneath them. Notice how you are able to feel your feet whilst also being able to read this page. Also become aware of any sounds going on around you. You will notice that is quite easy to continue reading, whilst also feeling your body resting on the ground and hearing sounds. In the same way we are able to focus on our Mindfulness support and also notice other activity going on within our mind and body, as well as in the environment around us.

Focusing lightly on our Mindfulness support; becoming distracted and lost in thinking; noticing this and gently bringing our attention back to resting on the Mindfulness support forms the majority of our Mindfulness practice. This is the Mindfulness technique. When we rest on our Mindfulness support, whilst being open to other aspects of our experience, we *know what is happening, while it is happening*. Then after a while we notice we are caught up in thinking and we return to the support. We recognise that our minds will wander repeatedly and that this is absolutely OK. Everyone's mind is like this, even after many years of Mindfulness practice.

It is best to set the expectation that most of our practice time will be spent distracted and then whenever we notice we have become distracted, we can celebrate an opportunity to practise Mindfulness and gently bring our attention back to focus lightly on the Mindfulness support. Many meditation teachers remark that it does not matter how many times we drift away and become distracted, the only important thing is to notice this and return to the support. That is how awareness grows. So we can see distraction as an opportunity instead of being a problem.

In fact the best expectation to set is that of being an epic failure! In this way we can practise our Mindfulness attitude of *without preference*, whether our experience is that of the mind wandering for the hundredth time in ten minutes, or whether our experience is that of completing the session without once remembering to be mindful. We all have sessions like this sometimes. We can train to be OK with whatever happens.

It is best to use one Mindfulness support during a given session, rather than moving around between different supports. The support we are going to explore first is sound.

Sound Support

Sometimes people believe that they need perfect conditions in order to practise Mindfulness meditation. We may think that we need a nice room, lovely cushions or a comfy chair, the right temperature and absolute silence. This is not the case, because our aim is to be mindful in daily life, in which circumstances are often far from perfect! Using sound as a support can dispel the idea that we need silence in order to practise.

When we use sound as a Mindfulness support the guidance is to let sounds come to us and not to go searching for sounds. So we are practising hearing not listening. We are not listening for particular sounds and we don't set up sounds, like music or chanting; instead we notice whatever sounds come and go around us. We also notice the gaps between sounds. Listening for sounds is active, whilst using a Mindfulness support of sound is more passive and receptive. This results in an expansive experience, as we are opening up to sounds arriving from the space surrounding us. Right now we can notice the sounds arriving at our ears and see what happens. For example, if we hear birdsong we often try to figure out what bird is singing or we may see an image of a bird in our mind. It can be interesting to notice our reactions to sounds as they emerge. Do we notice ourselves wanting to hold on to sounds that we perceive to be pleasant, such as birds singing? Do we notice ourselves wanting to get rid of sounds that we perceive to be unpleasant, such as a police siren.

We can explore whether it is possible to experience sound in a non-conceptual way as pure sensation of volume and pitch; experiencing sound as vibration. We can welcome loud sounds, silence and all that falls between these extremes. We can also welcome sounds from within the body and sounds from far in the distance and all sounds in-between.

It is important to bear in mind that using sound as a support is part of our overall practice routine of settling, grounding, resting and support. So when we are resting and find our attention drifting into thinking we notice this and lightly refocus our attention on hearing whatever sounds are occurring. This brings us back to where we are: mind resting in the body, body resting on the ground and attention lightly held by sound with an awareness of everything going on in and around us. So we always come back to grounding and resting. Using our rule of thumb, 20% of our attention is on sounds and 80% of our attention is on grounding and resting. So the focus on sound is not exclusive, as we are simultaneously aware of other aspects of our experience, such as body sensations, thoughts and emotions. In this way nothing is excluded from our Mindfulness practice.

We now have all the elements in place to try out the full practice routine: posture, intention and motivation, settling, grounding, resting, support and sharing. Remember that these practice instructions are merely a guide and once we familiarise ourselves with them we should make the practice our own.

Settling, Grounding, Resting and Support using Sound (or SGRS using Sound)

Follow the exercise written out below or follow the guided audio.

Do this exercise for around 20 minutes.

Start by placing your body in posture, alert, dignified and at ease. Then bring to mind your intention for this practice, for example, to be present in a kindly way. Next, reflect on your motivation for practising Mindfulness, for example, how you hope to benefit yourself and others from your Mindfulness practice.

Now focus in a relaxed way on your breath. Breathe in a little more deeply than normal, without strain, and then gently release the breath. Keeping the in- and out-breaths equal in length, you may find it useful to count to three or four on the in-breath and a similar count on the out-breath. Thoughts will continue to pop into your mind and this is totally normal. Let them go free, without attempting to suppress them or getting involved with them. After a few minutes focus a bit more on the out-breath, noticing any tendency for the body to relax as it releases the out-breath. Then let the breath return to its natural rhythm, letting go of the counting.

You may notice that by focusing on the out-breath your centre of gravity drops more fully into your body. This brings you into the phase of grounding. Now become aware of the weight of your body on the ground, and notice the points of touch and pressure as you sit on the chair or cushion: mind resting in the body like the body rests on the ground. Gradually broaden your focus to include sensations within the body, noticing how you feel from the inside. You can do this by scanning through the body systematically, or just opening to whatever sensations draw your attention. Then become aware of the space around your body, noticing that the body is resting on the ground with space all around.

This brings you into the phase of resting – being with your experience as it arises and passes, without any sense of doing or striving. Simply be aware of whatever arises through your senses without the need to think or react in any way – feeling sensations in the body, noticing thoughts, being in touch with emotions, and aware of sounds occurring in the space around you. If you find yourself reacting then just accept the reactions and in this way allow the mind to be open, alert and at rest.

When you notice that you have drifted off into thinking, gently refocus your attention on whatever sounds are occurring and let them hold your attention. This brings you back to where you are: mind resting in the body, and body resting on the ground. You may be aware of sounds far away or very close – even the sound of your own body breathing. Sounds may be loud or subtle; they may be experienced as pleasant or unpleasant; jarring or calming. They may be continuous or intermittent. Notice too the spaces between the sounds. See if you can experience sounds as pure sensation, without judging them and without getting caught up in thinking about them. You do not need to name what you are hearing, or to get caught up in thoughts of like or dislike. If you find that a sound has acted as a trigger into a train of thought, simply come back to hearing and let this be your anchor in the present moment. You do not need to chase after the sound or to push it away. You do not need to strain for sounds, but simply to notice what sounds come to you as you bring your focus to hearing. Perhaps you will be aware of other aspects of your experience as you focus on sound, such as thoughts, emotions or body sensations.

At the end of the practice, take some time to acknowledge the benefits that come from your Mindfulness practice. Then cultivate the wish to take this into your life and to share the benefits with those around you.

Three Stage Breathing Space

This practice is based on the three-minute breathing space, which was developed by Zindel Segal, Mark Williams and John Teasdale. It is a Mindfulness in Daily Life exercise from their Mindfulness-Based Cognitive Therapy (MBCT) program, which helps to build a bridge between our formal and our informal practice. It helps us to become mindful in daily life.

This practice is not about stepping out of daily life, but it is one of getting in touch with the moments in it. It enables us to move from 'doing mode' into 'being mode'.

In the first stage of the practice we adopt a posture that is alert, dignified and at ease, and we become mindful of the very moment we are in. We simply open up to our experience so as to 'know what is happening while it is happening, without preference'. We can notice what thoughts are arising in the mind or what we have been thinking about. We can notice whatever emotions are present for us just now and any physical sensations that we feel in the body. Once we are in touch with our present moment experience we can move on to the second stage. In this first stage our focus is wide.

In the second stage of the practice we narrow our focus to the detail of our breathing. We pay attention to the movement of the breath in and out of the body. Perhaps we can feel the breath brushing past the nostrils, feel the movement of our chest as each breath comes and goes, or feel the rising and falling of the belly with the breath. For a few breaths we can follow the whole path of the breath through the body from the nostrils down into the abdomen and then back out again. Once we feel grounded in the breath we can move on to the next stage.

In the third stage we gradually broaden our focus again, with a sense of allowing our experience to be just as is it. Starting from the breath we can widen our focus to become aware of our whole body, with a sense of allowing. We can widen further to notice activity within the mind, again with a sense of allowing our experience to be just as it is. Then we can widen our focus even more to open up to the environment surrounding the mind and body: the ground beneath our feet, the space around the body, sounds, the field of view before our eyes, and the whole of our experience in this moment.

Then we move into the next moments of our daily life with the intention of maintaining the energy of being mindful.

To start with we will do the three stage breathing space three times a day at set times, as a way of becoming familiar with the practice. Again, we may encounter the same challenge as we did with the Mindfulness in daily life tasks, which is how to remember to do the three stage breathing space. To remedy this, we can set alarms on our phones or computers at set times to remind us to do the practice. We can place prompts, such as stickers or notes, in the places we intend to do the practice as a reminder. It might be useful to be creative about how we remember and we may have to change our prompts every once in a while when we get used to them and no longer notice them. If we work in a busy office, we may feel a bit self-conscious about doing the practice at our desk. In this case it may be a good idea to do the practice during our trips to the loo, as we are in private and it is somewhere that we go regularly!

Once we are familiar with the practice, then we can do it when we experience moments of difficulty or even moments of joy. Often in life, especially in difficult situations, we do not have three minutes to spare, but we can use the outline of the practice as a way of being in touch with those moments. We can quickly check in with how we are: thoughts, emotions and sensations, then take a few mindful breaths and then open out our focus again to be in touch with all of our experience in this moment. Again, if things are getting tough, we can take ourselves off to the loo and do the practice there, and then come back feeling more ready to face the difficulty. In this way we can respond more skilfully to difficult moments, rather than reacting on autopilot and following our habitual patterns.

Also, we don't want to gloss over the joyful experiences in our lives and so we can do the practice then, as a way of really getting in touch with and appreciating these moments of joy that we can so easily miss.

Three Stage (or Three Minute) Breathing Space Practice

Follow the exercise written out below or follow the guided audio.

Do this exercise for around 3 to 5 minutes.

1. *WHAT'S HERE? – GETTING IN TOUCH – Notice your posture. Straighten your spine and generally relax the body. With your eyes either open or closed, silently ask yourself: "What is my experience right now, in my thoughts, my feelings, and my bodily sensations?" See if you can recognise and accept your experience, even if it is uncomfortable.*

2. *BREATHING – GATHERING – Then, gently redirect your full attention to your breathing, to each in-breath and to each out-breath as they follow, one after the other. Try noting at the back of your mind: "Breathing in... breathing out" or counting the breaths.*

3. *EXPANDING OUTWARDS – Open the field of your awareness around your breathing. Allow your attention to expand to the whole body – including any sense of discomfort, tension, or resistance. If these sensations are there, then bring your awareness to them by breathing into them on the in-breath. Then, breathe out from those sensations, softening and opening with the out-breath. Then broaden your focus to gradually include the whole of your experience. If you wish, you can say to yourself, "It's OK. Whatever it is, it's OK. Let me feel it. It is here already, so let me be present for it."*

As best you can, move mindfully into the next moments of your day.

Posture Sitting on a Cushion

Many people prefer to do their Mindfulness practice sitting in a chair. However, others prefer to sit on the floor to do their practice, either in a crossed-legged or kneeling position.

The same guidelines apply as for sitting in a chair and we select a posture that embodies the qualities of our practice:

- Alert
- Open
- Grounded
- Dignified
- At ease, embodying kindness to ourselves

When sitting on the floor, use one or more meditation cushions or a meditation stool to raise your buttocks off the floor, while keeping your knees close to the ground, with the knees lower than the buttocks.

If you are sitting cross-legged place your legs in front of you with one heel drawn towards your body in front of the middle of the groin and the other heel placed directly in front of the first heel, so that one leg is not resting on the other leg. If your knees are raised off the ground then place small cushions or rolled-up blankets underneath them, so that they are fully supported. Also, have some padding underneath your feet.

If you are kneeling then sit on a meditation stool or a pile of cushions with your feet behind you. Place some padding underneath your lower legs and feet and make sure that the stool or cushions are high enough so that the bend at the knee is not so sharp as to be uncomfortable.

It is most important to be comfortable and to be able to sit upright, with the spine erect, but not rigid, and with the chin slightly tucked in. Your upper arms should be slightly away from your body, as if you have an egg placed under each armpit, so as to give your chest space to be open and to breathe.

Place your hands palms down on your knees or place your hands palms up in your lap with one hand on top of the other hand and with the thumbs touching. See which is more comfortable. If possible, keep your eyes slightly open with a relaxed downward gaze.

It may be useful to experiment with a variety of stools or cushions before making a purchase. Perhaps you can visit a meditation centre and try a few different options. Attending yoga classes can help with posture and can enable you to get advice on how to sit in an upright and comfortable posture that suits your body.

Remember that to start with you might only be able to sit comfortably for five minutes or so. This is absolutely fine and you can switch posture, for example moving between a cushion and a chair, when you become uncomfortable, rather than sitting in pain. Gradually you can build up the length of time that you can sit comfortably in your chosen posture.

Practice Schedule for the Week after Session Three

Formal Practice

Alternate doing the bodyscan practice with the SGRS with sound support practice. You can use the guided audio from the MBLC app or on the webpage listed on page 6. At the end of the practice, reflect on what happened during your period of practice and make notes below. In particular, notice where your mind wandered to. Do this each day this week. This is your own personal record.

Day 1

_____

_____

_____

Day 2

_____

_____

_____

Day 3

_____

_____

_____

Day 4

_____

_____

_____

Day 5

_____

_____

_____

Day 6

_____

_____

_____

Day 7

_____

_____

_____

Informal Daily Life Practice

Do the three-minute breathing space three times a day, each day this week. Write here how you are going to remember to do it:

_____

_____

Continue with your previous daily life activity and add another one. Write here what your new daily life activity is going to be:

_____

_____

Describe below what you noticed when doing your informal daily life practice:

Day 1

_____

_____

_____

Day 2

_____

_____

_____

Day 3

_____

_____

Day 4

_____

_____

Day 5

_____

_____

_____

Day 6

_____

_____

_____

Day 7

_____

Chapter 5

Session Four – Working with Distraction

In this session we will explore one of the biggest obstacles to our mindfulness practice: becoming distracted by engaging with thought and getting lost in thinking. Before doing so, however, we will introduce another important practice: mindful movement.

Mindful Movement

Going back to our definition of Mindfulness, we practise *'knowing what is happening while it is happening'* while we are moving the body. In this way the movements of the body are a support to help us stay present. Then, when we notice that the mind has wandered we gently bring it back to noticing how it feels to move the body. This is our main technique in practising mindful movement.

We also practise *'without preference'*, which means that we allow our experience to be as it is in a kind and gentle way. We practise being curious about the body, being kind towards the limitations and weaknesses of the body, and we learn to trust the body as a place to be present.

Building on our experience of the bodyscan, we practise mindful movement as a way of connecting mind and body. When we begin practising Mindfulness many of us discover how disconnected we are from our bodies and we may even find it difficult to notice how the body is feeling. Mindful movement allows us to be more in touch with sensations in the body and to sense how the body feels on a moment-by-moment basis. When we experience an emotion, for example, we can recognise that something has changed in the body and this can wake us up to paying attention to our experience in that moment. The body generally tells us more accurately what emotion we are experiencing than our thinking mind. It tends to be in touch with the truth of our experience in the present moment, whereas the thinking mind is often out of touch with the present and is inclined to get lost in stories that obscure the truth of what is actually occurring.

Mindful movement is also an interesting practice for noticing how our habitual patterns of thinking play themselves out. For example, many of us have a habit of striving and so we might find ourselves trying to do a perfect movement, rather than just being aware of whatever movement we manage to do. Also, if we struggle with doing a particular movement, we might fall into the habit of criticising ourselves and telling ourselves that we are not good enough, rather than simply accepting our bodily limitations as part of the practice. In this way, mindful movement clearly reveals our habitual patterns of thought, and once we see them we are no longer at their mercy. This body of ours works very hard to keep us moving through our lives and we often take this for granted. Mindful movement gives us an opportunity to be grateful for our body and to appreciate all that it does for us. Many of us will have bodies that are limited in some way, perhaps through wear and tear, illness or injury. In this case, we can learn to acknowledge and come to terms with these limitations in a kind way and to appreciate what our body can do, rather than always wishing it to be different.

Mindful movement also acts as a bridge into daily life because our daily life activities invariably involve movement. Through becoming aware of the range and feel of the body's movements in mindful movement practice, we can develop a habit that will naturally carry through into daily life. We will find ourselves becoming more intimately aware of our body and how it moves. Then gradually, over time, we will find that we are more in touch with the poignancy and preciousness of our lives as they unfold moment-by-moment.

It is useful to remember that mindful movement is a formal Mindfulness practice and so it can be done as an alternative to Mindfulness sitting practice or bodyscan. Furthermore, many of us already practise movement during our lives, for example walking, playing a sport, running, cycling, yoga or swimming. We can choose to do these activities mindfully and make them part of our formal Mindfulness practice.

A deeper dimension of mindful movement is *'working the edge'* with uncomfortable physical sensations. For example, we might hold our arms above our heads and notice how physical sensations build up to a point where the posture becomes uncomfortable. Then we can imagine breathing in to the discomfort on each in-breath and breathing out from the area of discomfort on each out-breath, as a way of welcoming the discomfort as part of our experience. We can notice how our experience of the discomfort subtly changes and then notice the process that goes on in our minds as we decide when to lower our arms.

We practise *'working the edge'* with physical sensations as a way of preparing to work with uncomfortable emotional feelings that may arise during our Mindfulness practice. This is because physical discomfort can often be easier to be with than emotional discomfort, such as feelings of anger, sadness or shame. We may have been trying to avoid emotional discomfort for a long time, by distracting ourselves with work or television, or by overeating or drinking too much alcohol. One aim of Mindfulness practice is gradually to face and get to know these emotions, so that we are no longer controlled by them. *'Working the edge'* helps to bring us to this point.

We now introduce two mindful movement practices, one is a yoga-based movement practice and the other is mindful walking.

Yoga Based Mindful Movement

Follow the exercise written out below or follow the guided audio.

Do this exercise for around 20 to 30 minutes.

When following this mindful movement practice, remember that YOU are the expert of your own body and know better than anyone else what movements are OK and what movements are not OK for your body to do. It is important to take responsibility for your body and to look after it during mindful movement practice. Also, while doing the movements breathe gently through your nostrils, if that is comfortable for you.

Corpse pose - lying down on back, arms by sides, back of neck long, legs either straight with feet flopped apart or legs bent with knees propped together and feet apart. Offer the alternative of sitting in a chair. Notice contact between body and floor and then move attention to breathing gently through nostrils, then notice abdomen rising and falling.

Dynamic bridge pose - have the knees bent and feet on the floor, with your knees and feet a hip's distance apart and your arms by your sides. Curl your back up off the floor and then curl back down. To do this tilt your pubic bone upwards, with your low back pushed into the floor and then lift your bottom and then your low back up off the floor, then lower by pushing the low back into the floor before finally lowering the bottom. Keep the back of your neck long. Notice how the movement feels. Offer the alternative of sitting in a chair and alternately rounding the back and then straightening the back and opening the chest.

Wind relieving pose - bring the knees, one first and then the other, into the chest, hold the back of the thighs and rock knees gently forwards and backwards and then from side to side. Notice any change in contact between the low back and the floor.

Transition

Roll onto one side and gently move into a sitting position, with your legs in front of you and apart. If it is difficult to sit with a straight spine with the legs straight, then bend the knees and place a blanket or cushion under your knees for support. It may help you to sit straight with a yoga block or a cushion under your tail bone and with your sitting bones on the floor so as to tilt the pelvis forward.

Shoulder rolls - roll the shoulders forwards and then backwards, exploring the range of movement in your shoulders, and feeling from the inside the patterns of sensation you experience.

Seated twist - with your hands on your chest and a long spine, turn your ribcage, then shoulders and then neck to the left side, keeping the hips pointing forwards. Each time you breathe in lengthen the spine and as you breathe out ease into the twist. Come back to centre and then repeat to the right side.

Seated forward bend - with your hands on your chest, lengthen the spine as you breathe in and tilt forwards from the hips, keeping the spine straight and the chest open as you breathe out.

81

A small amount of movement is fine. Then place your hands on your knees and allow the spine to curve forwards and allow head to drop. Notice where you feel a stretch. Then come back to an upright position.

Transition

Prepare for a Move mindfully from sitting to standing.

Mountain pose - stand with your feet a hip's distance apart, with your arms by your sides. Knees are very slightly bent, pelvis is tucked under (opposite movement to sticking bottom out), stomach muscles engaged, lengthen between the hips and the ribcage, lift the chest, lengthen the spine, relax the shoulders with the back of the neck long. Notice the predominant sensations in your body. Offer the option of sitting.

Prepare for a
balance

Keep your gaze on a spot in front of you or on the floor to help you balance. Move your weight forwards into the balls of your feet, then back into your heels. Move your weight into your left foot and then your right foot. Tune into the changing feelings of contact between your feet and the floor. Come back to a central balanced position with the weight evenly distributed between the left and right foot and the balls and heels of the feet. Offer the option to stay sitting and imagining the weight shifting.

Tree pose - Take your arms out to the side to help you to balance. Shift your weight to the right foot and lift the left foot and place it on the right foot or calf, with the left knee out to the side. Notice the small movements in your right foot and ankle as you balance. Repeat to the other side. For those who are sitting offer the option of imagining doing the balance.

Dynamic palm tree pose - Take the feet a bit further apart and have your arms by your sides. With a straight spine as you breathe out lean to the left side and turn your head to the right, as you breathe in come back to centre and lengthen the spine. Repeat to the other side and then to alternate sides. Offer the option of doing this sitting.

Seaweed exercise - With the feet firmly grounded into the floor, imagine you are seaweed in a stormy sea, moving the upper body from side to side and waving your arms above your head. Gradually the storm abates and the movements become smaller until eventually you come back to stillness with your arms by your sides. Offer the option of doing this sitting.

Tune in to your body. Notice if there is any way in which it feels it would like to move and then mindfully move in this way. Noticing how the movement feels.

Mountain pose to end.

Mindful Walking

Follow the exercise written out below.

Do this exercise for around 20 to 30 minutes.

Begin by standing in an erect and dignified posture, with the spine upright; the arms by the side of the body and the knees slightly bent. Now reflect on your intention for this practice, perhaps to be present and to notice the experience of walking with kindly curiosity. Now reflect on your motivation for practising Mindfulness: perhaps to benefit yourself and those around you in some way.

When you practise walking meditation, you do not need to be going anywhere, and it can be helpful to let go of any sense of a destination or a purpose to the walking. The intention of walking meditation is just to walk!

You can let your body do the walking, trusting that the body knows what to do. You do not need to guide it with the mind. You can just allow the mind to observe and then gently notice the changing flow of experience. You can simply enjoy your walking.

When you practise walking meditation, you practise bringing awareness to the whole experience of walking: the lifting and placing of the feet; the sensations of the soles of the feet touching the ground; the shifting sensations of pressure and touch; the shift in balance of the body from one side to the next; the movements throughout the whole body as we move; and the flowing of the breath. There will also be awareness of the space in which you move, the varying surfaces upon which you step, the touch of the air on your skin, the changing views, sounds and smells coming through your senses: moment-to-moment experiences, constantly flowing and changing.

There will be moments when you will notice that your mind has wandered into thinking, perhaps distracted by some of the sense experiences, or by some inner thought activities. Just as you would in the other Mindfulness practices, simply acknowledge the fact that you are distracted, and gently bring your awareness back to the walking:

... lifting and placing; lifting and placing; breathing in and

breathing out.

Walking meditation can be practised slowly and purposefully, and can involve choosing a path where you may walk back and forth, or in a circle. It can also be practised at a natural pace when you are going about your life: walking down the corridors in your place of work; walking through the car park; walking through a busy high street or down the aisles in the supermarket.

Working with Distraction

Set a timer for three minutes and then sit with the intention to be present, not using any technique or Mindfulness support to stay present.

Write down here what happened and if your mind wandered write down where it wandered to:

_____

_____

_____

For most of us, if we sit for a few minutes with nothing to do, we find ourselves caught up in thinking very quickly. What we find ourselves thinking about will very much depend on our habits.

Distraction in the Past, Present and Future

Many of us have a habit of ruminating over past events, in particular upsetting events that didn't go the way we wanted. We labour under the misapprehension that there is a simple answer to fix, justify or understand this event, if only we can think about it enough. In thinking about difficult events over and over again, we tend to re-experience the emotions of the event and may experience a sense of failure over and over again. This can make us dissatisfied, unhappy and miserable. We are doing this to ourselves a lot of the time, tormenting ourselves by revisiting painful memories. This is a common human tendency, through which we unwittingly reinforce negative emotions and self-pity, which hurts us but doesn't resolve anything. This is distraction into the past and it can lead to stress and low mood.

Many of us daydream, thinking about something we perceive to be pleasant in order to escape from the present moment, particularly if the present moment is painful or boring. This is a habit of avoiding and supressing difficulty, which is a temporary solution, as the difficulty will only come back to haunt us again in the future. Then there are those of us who have a habit of constantly analysing and trying to figure things out, uncomfortable with any hint of not knowing. A big part of our Mindfulness training is learning to be OK with not knowing. There are many things that we cannot know for certain. These are examples of distraction in the present.

Many of us have a habit of worrying and feeling anxious about what might happen in the future. Here, we labour under the misapprehension that there is a simple answer to our future, which we will find if only we can think about it enough. In reality life is more complex, with innumerable causes and conditions influencing how the future will unfold, most of which are beyond our control, such that no simple answer will suffice. Perhaps we feel insecure about a future endeavour or have a desire to be in control of what happens in the future. This can lead to distraction into the future, where we find ourselves endlessly planning, anticipating problems, or catastrophising about what might happen. While it can be useful to plan for the future, if we have a habit of doing this endlessly and planning for worst-case scenarios, this can lead to feelings of anxiety and insecurity. Not only are these feelings unnecessary, they can also lead to stress and low mood.

Many of us have all of these habits of distraction, past, present and future, which lead us to think about the same things over and over again, convinced that there is some sort of answer or solution to fix what is wrong with us and our life. Albert Einstein had a definition of insanity, which is:

Doing the same thing over and over again and expecting a different answer.

Yet still we are convinced that if we think about this problem for the 100th time we will get the right answer!

Where do we find the answers to our life's problems? Do they come from thinking about them endlessly? Or do these answers arise spontaneously, when the mind is given some space to rest from endlessly thinking? We might even find that things fall clearly into place when we are doing the washing up, or are out for a run or a walk. Sometimes there are no answers to life's complex problems and the wisest course of action is just to keep going.

What is Distraction?

Distraction is the natural impulse of the mind to move away from the present moment. The mind does this by engaging with thoughts that arise within the mind and getting caught up in thinking. Distraction is a habit. We have spent most of our lives in the habit of distraction, always thinking about something. Our education and culture encourages this and places little value on quiet time or reflection. Recall the principle 'energy follows focus'. If we spend much of our time thinking about things, then this is where we place our focus and then we feed more energy into the habit of thinking. In our Mindfulness practice we are repeatedly withdrawing our focus from thinking activity and generating a new habit of being present, in which we are aware of thoughts, but are not caught up in them.

It is important not to beat ourselves up about this strong habit of distraction because it is part of the human condition. We have evolved to be distracted and always on the lookout. In fact, there is a part of the brain called the *default mode network* that is constantly scanning and processing information coming through the senses, always on the alert for threats and things we might want to acquire. So it is important to accept the fact that we are hardwired to be distracted, but at the same time we can work with this situation. Our task is simply to notice where the mind has wandered to and to come back again and again to our Mindfulness support. In this way we train our focus to be in the present moment, while at the same time becoming curious about distraction. We can assist this process by softly naming where our attention drifts away to, such as 'planning, future conversation, past memory, fantasy' etc, before we come back to the Mindfulness support. Research shows that practising Mindfulness calms down the *default mode network*.

More and more we see that there is nothing wrong with distraction. In fact, distraction is like a teacher because it shows us where our attention habitually goes and where we invest so much of our mental energy. In the Tibetan tradition meditation is defined as becoming familiar with the mind and how it moves. So distractions are a big part of our learning about the mind. For this reason it is important to make friends with distraction. When we do this we see that distraction occurs on a spectrum, from being completely lost in thought on the one hand to one-pointed focus on the support on the other hand. Most of the time we are somewhere on this spectrum, perhaps partially distracted, but at the same time maintaining a thread of Mindfulness.

Becoming Worse

After we have been practising Mindfulness for a few weeks, we may begin to notice that our mind is full of distractions that didn't seem to be there before. This can lead to a perception that our Mindfulness practice is not working and that our inner state of confusion and distraction is becoming worse! In fact this is a good sign. It is a sign that our awareness is growing stronger. When we first start to practise our level of awareness is weak so we might only notice the most obvious level of thinking activity. As our Mindfulness strengthens, however, we begin to notice more subtle levels of thinking activity and deeper currents of distraction within the mind. What we previously experienced as a peaceful mind can begin to feel very busy and chaotic and we might well think we are getting worse. It is important to reassure ourselves at this stage that we are on the right track and to remember that Mindfulness is not about finding a peaceful state of mind to dwell in; it is about seeing more clearly what has been there all of the time. Once we are willing to see what is there from a place of acceptance and not become involved in what we see, a deeper level of settling takes place, and the seeds are sown for a more authentic experience of inner peace.

Breath Support

So far in our training we have used the body as a Mindfulness support in the bodyscan and mindful movement practices. We have used sound as a Mindfulness support. We have also used regulating the breath and counting, during settling the mind. Now we move on to using the natural rhythm of breathing as a Mindfulness support.

When we use the breath as a support, after settling, grounding and resting, it is different from how we use the breath in settling. In settling we regulate the breath, but when we use breath as a support we do not change, control or regulate it in any way; we simply observe the breath as it naturally flows within the body. We let the breath breathe itself.

Using breath as a Mindfulness support is an embodied experience, because we are feeling the movement of the breath within the body. So when we use breath as a support, we remain connected to the stage of grounding (in settling, grounding, resting and support) and feel the weight of the body on the ground and how the breath moves in the body: mind resting in the body like the body rests on the ground, with our attention lightly focused on the breathing wherever we notice it most easily in the body.

We might feel the breath at the nose, as the breath brushes over our upper lip and past the insides of our nostrils. This can be quite a subtle feeling. It may even be possible to feel the relative coolness of the breath moving into the body through the nostrils, compared to the relative warmth of the breath as it moves out of the body.

Alternatively, we can choose to feel the breath in the chest, as the chest expands and contracts with each breath. We might feel sensations of movement in the chest at the front or the sides of the ribcage. We may notice more subtle sensations of expanding and contracting movements at the back of the ribcage or in the region of the collarbones.

It can be grounding to feel the breath in the belly. Each time we breathe in we might feel the gentle expansion of the belly and each time we breathe out we might feel a gentle contraction. To start with it can be helpful to place the hands on the belly so as to tune in to this movement and to notice how it feels. We can tune in to the detailed patterns of physical sensations that arise and fall with the rhythmical movement of the belly.

Alternatively, we can feel the full passage of the breath through the body. The passing of the breath over the nostrils and down the throat, and then the rising of the chest and belly followed by the falling of the chest and belly, and the passing of the breath up the throat and out through the nostrils.

We can each explore the different movements of the breath through the body and see where our focus naturally rests on the breath: nostrils, chest or belly.

For some of us attending to the breath can cause the breath to become laboured and make us feel anxious. In this case continue to use sound as a Mindfulness support. We can make an intention to come back to using breath as a support at a later time, when our Mindfulness practice is more established.

Working with Distraction

We can now use the principles we explored earlier in working with distraction when we use the breath as a Mindfulness support. Every time we discover that our attention has drifted off into thinking or dreaming, we notice where our mind has gone: dwelling on the past, worrying about the future or thinking about the present. For some people gentle labelling enhances this sense of curiosity. We then gently refocus our attention on the breathing, not in the sense of wrenching away from thought, but lightly refocusing on the breath wherever we feel it most easily in the body. This light touch is important and also the attitude that the distractions are welcome; they are not the enemy. When our attention comes back to the breathing, we are brought back to where we are: sitting on the chair or cushion. We always come back to the grounding and resting: the sense of our mind landing back in the body and being with (or resting with) whatever is present in our experience now.

As our practice develops we get an 'embodied feel' of what distraction is like. There is a moment of loss of awareness as we find ourselves carried away in a thought-stream. The sense of spaciousness is gone, because our mind homes in on the story we are lost in. The sense of grounding is also gone, because distraction tends to take us out of the body. When we notice this we get used to the feeling of regaining Mindfulness. Intention is what wakes us up from the dream of distraction; we remember that we are trying to practise Mindfulness. This is the aspect of recollection. Then there is the moment of curiosity, as we notice what habitual pathway we have once more travelled down. Next, there is the moment of refocusing on the breathing, which brings us back to the body, back to grounding. This in turn brings us back to the simple experience of being with what we are feeling in that moment, and this opens up the space that was always there, in and around what we are experiencing. It brings us back to the phase of resting. So we get used to the feeling of being distracted and we get used to the feeling of regaining Mindfulness. This is how awareness grows. It does not happen in a neat and tidy way, by holding the mind tight in the zone of peace; instead it happens through the messy process of losing awareness and then finding it again.

Settling, Grounding, Resting and Mindfulness Support using Breath

Follow the exercise written out below or follow the guided audio.

Do this exercise for around 20 to 30 minutes.

Start by placing your body in posture: alert, dignified and at ease. Then bring to mind your intention for this practice, for example, to be present in a kindly way. Then reflect on your motivation for practising Mindfulness, for example, how you hope to benefit yourself and others from your Mindfulness practice.

Then focus in a very relaxed way on your breath. Breathe in a little more deeply than normal, without strain, and then gently releasing the breath. Keep the in- and out-breaths equal in length, you may find it useful to count to three or four on the in-breath and a similar count on the out-breath. Thoughts will continue to pop into your mind and this is totally normal. Let them go free, without attempting to suppress or get involved with them. After a few minutes focus a bit more on the out-breath and notice any tendency for the body to relax as it releases the out-breath. Then let the breath return to its natural rhythm and let go of the counting.

You may notice that by focusing on the out-breath your centre of gravity drops more fully into your body. This brings you into the phase of grounding. Now become aware of the weight of your body on the ground, and notice the points of touch and pressure as you sit on the chair or cushion: mind resting in the body like the body rests on the ground. Gradually broaden your focus to include sensations within the body, noticing how you feel in the body. You can do this by scanning through the body systematically, or just opening to whatever sensations draw your attention. Then become aware of the space around your body, noticing that the body is resting on the ground with space all around.

This brings you into the phase of resting – being with your experience as it arises and passes without any sense of doing or striving. Simply be aware of whatever arises through your senses without the need to think or react in any way – feeling sensations in the body, noticing thoughts, being in touch with emotions, and aware of sounds occurring in the space around you. If you find yourself reacting then just be with the reactions; in this way allowing the mind to be open, alert and at rest.

When you notice that you have become engaged in thinking, this is the point where you work with the support of breathing. Gently refocus your attention on your breathing and on how the breath moves in your body – how you inhabit a breathing body. You can notice the expansion and contraction of the belly, the chest or the ribcage, or you can feel the entry and exit point of the breath at the tip of the nostrils. You can rest your attention at a point in the body where the breath is felt most vividly, or you can follow an entire breath cycle, riding the waves of the breath, noting its flow and its changing qualities.

Be aware of any tendency to want to control or change the breath, simply allowing the breathing to happen in its own way. You can let yourself simply surrender to the breath, as if you are letting yourself 'be breathed'. Each time the mind wanders, and you recognise this fact, you gently and kindly bring yourself back to the breathing. This is the core of the practice. You are cultivating qualities of patience, perseverance and concentration, with a kindly acceptance towards yourself and your experience.

Again and again, you will notice that your attention has drifted into thinking, and has left the sensations of the breath. You will notice that there are many places that the mind likes to go to: the past, the future, worries, planning, judging, evaluating, commentating, fantasising – a vast variety of random thinking activity. As soon as you notice that the mind is no longer with the breath, you can congratulate yourself for waking up! This is a moment of Mindfulness. There is no need to judge yourself – it is in the nature of the mind to wander and you are learning more about how the mind is addicted to distraction. Simply acknowledge the fact that you have been thinking, and gently – but firmly – escort your attention back to the breath, again and again and again.

Practice Schedule for the Week after Session Four

Formal Practice

Alternate doing the mindful movement practice or mindful walking practice with SGRS, with breath support practice. You can use the guided audio from the MBLC app or on the webpage listed on page 6. At the end of the practice, reflect on what happened during your period of practice and make notes below. In particular, notice any distractions. Where was your mind drawn to: past, present, future? Also notice any particular patterns of distraction.

Day 1

_____

_____

_____

Day 2

_____

_____

Day 3

Day 4

Day 5

Day 6

Day 7

_____

_____

Informal Daily Life Practice

Do the three stage breathing space three times a day, each day this week. Write here any problems you had remembering to do this practice last week and any new plans for how you are going to remember to do it this week:

_____

_____

_____

_____

Continue with your previous daily life activities and again add another one. Write here what your new daily life activity is going to be:

_____

_____

Describe below what you noticed when doing your informal daily life practice:

Day 1

_____

_____

_____

Day 2

_____

_____

_____

Day 3

_____

_____

_____

Day 4

_____

_____

_____

Day 5

_____

_____

_____

Day 6

_____

_____

_____

Day 7

_____

_____

_____

Chapter 6

Session Five – Exploring the Undercurrent

In this chapter we introduce the Undercurrent and Observer model to help us navigate the inner processes of the mind when we practise Mindfulness. It is important to remember, however, that this is just a model to gain insight into certain activities of the mind. Whilst it is not put forward as a complete theory, this model is very helpful in clarifying which part of the mind can be trained when we engage in Mindfulness practice and where change takes place.

If we go back to our definition of Mindfulness – *knowing what is happening, while it is happening, without preference* – then the Undercurrent is what is happening and the Observer is that which can know what is happening.

We notice from our Mindfulness practice that two processes are taking place:

- Thought activity (undercurrent)
- Awareness of thought activity (observer)

We generally experience this in terms of 'me' and 'my thoughts'. Thoughts are happening within the mind and there is a sense of a 'me' who knows that these thoughts are happening. The 'me' who knows then characterises the thoughts as 'my thoughts'. 'My thoughts' are the undercurrent, and the sense of a 'me' that knows these thoughts are happening is the observer. In this chapter we focus on the undercurrent and in the next chapter we look more closely at the observer.

Pink elephant exercise

Set a timer for five minutes and then sit down and try not to think of pink elephants, until the time is up. Don't use any technique to keep the mind present, but just let the mind go free, all the while trying not to think of pink elephants.

Now write down here what you noticed during the five minutes:

_____

_____

_____

_____

_____

When asked to do this exercise many people find themselves thinking about not only pink elephants, but also elephants and other creatures of many different colours, such as blue unicorns and green hippos! This is an example of the activity of the undercurrent.

The undercurrent is the constant flow of thought activity that occurs within the mind: thoughts, images, memories, tunes and repetitive storylines. There are different layers to the undercurrent: some are superficial like thoughts of pink elephants, while other currents of thought and emotion run deep. We do not choose this background chatter, and yet it arises. For this reason it is involuntary. This is an important point because it means that we cannot control the undercurrent by direct intervention. We can't simply put a stop to it. When some people start meditating and come face-to-face with the undercurrent, there might be a feeling of dismay and a wish to make the mind go blank to stop all these crazy thoughts! But this simply does not work; it is like trying to stop the wind blowing or clouds from appearing in the sky. All we will end up doing is suppressing our thinking and emotional activity with the result that it will come up in another area of our lives. For this reason we need to find a different way of working with the undercurrent.

We call it the 'undercurrent' because it flows just beneath the level of our normal mind activity, i.e. what we are intentionally focusing on at any given moment. An example of the difference between these two levels of mind is attending a business meeting. We might be very clear and focused when we are present in the meeting, and be pleased with ourselves for negotiating a good deal. This is normal mind focus. Once the meeting is over, however, as we walk back to our car and drive home, we might find our awareness dropping down into an irrational stream of random thoughts, images and emotions that are anything but clear! This is the undercurrent – and we all have one. If you walk down any city street and look at people's faces, you may notice that they are lost in thinking and not really present, as though they are lost in a dream. If you then catch someone's attention and greet them, you might detect a moment in which they regain awareness. It's as if they wake up from the spell of the undercurrent – and quickly shift back into normal mind focus, when a few moments earlier they might have been immersed in an entirely different inner world of random thoughts, images and emotions.

The reason why we are focusing on the undercurrent is because we constantly get involved with it. We are constantly feeding this crazy stream of internal chatter. It is like falling into a river and allowing ourselves to be carried along by it. Through Mindfulness practice we learn to notice when we fall in and we use a Mindfulness support to help us step out of the water and sit on the bank, simply watching it flow by. Without this training we find ourselves constantly falling in and being carried along. This is problematic because we then unwittingly feed many patterns of thought and emotion that are negative and unhealthy – and in many cases very destructive. We explored this earlier with the principle of 'energy follows focus': what we feed grows, and so if we feed negative habits, they grow.

In fact most of us are obsessed with the undercurrent. It is as if there is a part of the mind that is constantly monitoring what is 'coming up' and it does so with a strong sense of preference: do I like these feeling and images arising, and if so how can I prolong them? Or how can I get rid of these unpleasant feelings and associated thoughts? Rob Nairn refers to this as "content obsession" – being fixated on what is arising in the undercurrent from moment-to-moment, and doing whatever we can to hold on to, develop, fix, get rid of, or sanitise the undercurrent. It might be useful to reflect on how much time you spend battling with the undercurrent in this way, and then ask yourself the question: does this go anywhere?

In the next chapter we will explore the part of the mind that is constantly monitoring the undercurrent with preference. However, we need to start by becoming more familiar with what is arising in the undercurrent moment-by-moment. It is important to do this because we seldom look directly at the undercurrent and see clearly what is there. Instead we tend to be seduced into its crazy ramblings through lapsing into unawareness, and then it just carries us along in its eddies and currents.

An everyday example of noticing the undercurrent is when someone asks you the question, "How are you?" You may say, "Fine," which is sometimes the polite thing to say, even if it isn't true. Or you might spend a few moments checking in with what thoughts and feelings you are experiencing just then. In doing this, your observer is examining the content of your undercurrent. Let's now do an exercise to help us become aware of what is arising in our undercurrent. It is important to keep this inquiry more experiential than theoretical, because its purpose is to clarify how we are relating to our inner experience.

Noticing the Undercurrent

Follow the exercise written out below or follow the guided audio.
Do this exercise for around 20 minutes.

Start with the intention to stay present and to notice the thoughts arising in your undercurrent. Then spend a few moments reflecting on your motivation for doing this; perhaps to understand better why you compulsively engage with thinking. Then move on to settling, grounding, resting, and breath or sound as a support.

Focus on your chosen Mindfulness support in a very relaxed way being careful not to obstruct thoughts. In fact, develop an interest in the fact that thoughts keep arising. Learn to watch them, so that gradually the existence of the undercurrent becomes clear to you. Then each time you notice that you have become caught up in thinking (i.e. engaging with thoughts), simply notice where the mind has wandered to and then gently return your attention to your Mindfulness support. Once you are settled back on the Mindfulness support, begin to notice the arising of thoughts once again.

Every now and again switch your attention to the stream of thoughts, images or background chatter moving through your awareness, and make it your support for 20 to 30 seconds, and then return to your chosen Mindfulness support.

Towards the end of your practice session, reflect on the following questions and make some notes in your reflective journal:

- *What kinds of thoughts were present?*
- *Were they conceptual thoughts, images or storylines?*
- *Did you notice an emotional charge behind them?*
- *Did they remain or did they move on and change?*
- *What happened to them when you did not engage with them?*
- *Where did they go?*

By doing this exercise we might begin to see that little new arises in the undercurrent. It tends to replay the same themes and dramas, and again and again we find ourselves becoming involved with it. This is the result of our conditioning – our past experience: the type of content that arises in our undercurrent depends on it. For example, if we have done a lot of worrying in the past, it is likely that many thoughts of worry will arise in our undercurrent; a lot of time in the past spent thinking about sad things means it is likely that many sad thoughts will arise. Equally, if we have spent a lot of time in the past thinking about all the things in life we appreciate, it is likely that many appreciative thoughts will arise in our undercurrent. So the types of thoughts that tend to arise in our undercurrent are familiar to us, because they are an echo of the past. They are an expression of our old habitual patterns.

When we hear an echo, it is the result of a previous sound. In the same way the thoughts that arise within the undercurrent are the result of something that happened previously: a past stimulus or experience. This process is habitual and we experience it all the time. External events, such as a noise or a smell, can trigger a train of thoughts within the mind. For example, hearing some words of a song might trigger a thought relating to a memory. We don't choose to have this thought – it arises by itself. By the time we are thinking about the memory, the trigger is in the past.

The key point here is that the undercurrent is all about the past. It is an echo and there is little we can do about it once it arises. The only sane thing to do is to leave it alone. And yet, reflecting back to the exercise we just did, how often do we just leave it alone? More often than not we find ourselves trying to fix and control the undercurrent. We try to get rid of the thoughts we don't want to experience and to grasp hold of the thoughts we do want to experience. We have been doing this all our lives. But has it worked? If it had worked, then you probably wouldn't be reading this book! Once we shout in a mountainous valley, we cannot stop the echoes from coming back. Or once we throw a pebble into the air, we can't stop it from coming down. Similarly, once we feed energy into habitual patterns of thinking and feeling, we are powerless to stop experiencing thoughts and feelings emanating from them. For example, if we feed a tendency towards anger then we will experience angry thoughts. Once those angry thoughts arise there is little point in trying to fix, sanitise or suppress them. If we do this we end up feeding the habitual patterns that gave birth to them and this will cause them to arise even more strongly again.

This point lies at the heart of the Undercurrent and Observer model. Invariably, we focus our energies in the *wrong place* – trying to stop the effects once the causes have already been set in motion. This is not some abstract philosophical exercise; it is about seeing clearly how we create our suffering from moment-to-moment. We all know that feeling of battling with what is 'coming up' in ourselves, not wanting to feel it, even though in some deep part of ourselves we know that this goes nowhere!

We need to focus our energies in the right place, i.e. how the observer reacts to thoughts and feelings that arise, and the set of preferences that shape how the observer observes (more of this in the next chapter). The main point with the undercurrent is to *leave it alone*. When we do this we will notice it has three important characteristics:

- *The undercurrent is self-arising.* This means that thoughts pop into the mind of their own volition. We don't choose to have them. We sat trying not to think of pink elephants and yet what thoughts arose? Did we choose to think these thoughts or did they just pop into the mind of their own accord? The undercurrent is autonomous and involuntary. It is not under our control.

- *The undercurrent is self-displaying.* This means that if we leave the undercurrent alone it will show us all we need to know about the content that is arising. This is how insight arises – when we get out of the way and let the mind reveal its secrets! The *eureka* moments we experience in life often occur when we are not busy problem solving and analysing, but when we give up control.

- *The undercurrent is self-liberating.* This means that if we leave the content of the undercurrent alone it will fade away. We experience this all the time. We can be preoccupied with a thought that seems to be of great importance one moment and in the next moment that thought is gone. Again, the mind does this by itself.

This process is profoundly liberating. As the great meditation teacher Gendun Rinpoche put it: "Nothing to do, nowhere to go and everything happens by itself." We cannot directly train the undercurrent, but we can train to give the undercurrent complete freedom. We can give up any notion of trying to control the undercurrent. This is counter-intuitive, but the more we leave the undercurrent alone the more it will reveal itself to us. This begins a process of psychological insight which arises by itself and which gradually exposes and weakens our habitual patterns.

Rob Nairn often quotes Krishnamurti in saying:

The seeing is the doing.

Once we impartially observe our habitual patterns, without trying to suppress them or engage them, they lose their power over us. So we don't have to do any more than just 'seeing' our habitual patterns. This is because once our habitual patterns are seen with unconditional acceptance the 'doing' happens all by itself and we spontaneously find ourselves doing something different from our usual conditioned response.

Although we cannot directly train the undercurrent we can train the observer to relate differently to the content of the undercurrent. We will look at this in Chapter 7. In this way our training is one of training the observer to observe impartially, without preference and with unconditional acceptance. We will go on to explore acceptance in Chapter 8.

Loving-kindness

Cultivating an atmosphere of kindness within the mind is an important part of our training. This is especially important when we start becoming aware of the undercurrent and learning to work skilfully with it. Often the thoughts that arise within the undercurrent are charged with negative emotions, making them toxic and unpleasant, so if we don't train in kindness and acceptance then such thoughts can pull us down into a tailspin of rumination and self-criticism.

We began our training in kindness with the memories of kindness exercise in Session Two. Through doing this exercise we got a sense of how kindness flows in different directions:

- Flow of kindness from self to other – giving kindness to others
- Flow of kindness from other to self – receiving kindness from others
- Flow of kindness from self to self – being kind to ourselves

For many of us, receiving kindness from others can be tricky because it can open us up to feelings of vulnerability and weakness; and we may feel we owe something to the person who is kind to us, or are simply undeserving of another's kindness.

Many of us also struggle with being kind to ourselves, believing that if we are kind to ourselves we will become lazy and ineffectual. We may believe that we are not worthy of our own kindness, but even worse, that we deserve harsh self-judgment and criticism. It is important to remember that these feelings and attitudes arise from our social and family conditioning – they are not our fault.

In these circumstances, it is sensible to begin cultivating

loving-kindness towards a loved one, i.e. starting with the flow of kindness from self to others. Once we have established this, we see if we can open up the flow to include ourselves.

In choosing a loved one it is best to choose someone with whom we have a straightforward relationship – someone towards whom our heart opens naturally and easily when we bring them to mind. We might love our partner, our parents or our children very much, but our relationship with them might be quite complex and also include frustrations and resentments, as well as feelings of loving-kindness, so it is best to start with a simple relationship. Animals and pets can be good for this.

The practice involves imagining that this person or animal is present with us. We can imagine them sitting here with us and it may help to imagine that you offer a gesture of kindness to them, such as a hug or a kindly touch. We may have an image in the mind of this person or animal, or we may have a felt sense of them being here. An image does not have to be picture perfect or constant; it might be a flickering of images that come and go. Our minds work in different ways and we imagine in different ways. The key is to bring this person or animal to mind in whatever way works best for you.

The loving-kindness for other exercise presented here is based on the Buddhist practice of *metta bhavana* and includes repeating certain phrases. The traditional phrases include:

- May you be happy
- May you be healthy
- May you be safe
- May you live with ease

If these phrases don't work for you, then choose your own. We imagine our chosen person or animal in front of us and just notice what happens within our mind. We stay curious about any thoughts, emotions or physical sensations that arise. Then we begin saying the phrases for them and again notice what happens. There is no right or wrong way to experience this practice. We simply notice the way in which our experience unfolds.

It is important to practise loving-kindness in an embodied way, and to stay grounded and in touch with any physical sensations that arise within the body. These may be sensations of warmth or kindness, shutting down or numbness, or sensations associated with an emotion, such as anger or sadness. Our practice is to welcome whatever feelings arise. Again, there is no right or wrong way to feel in this practice.

Sometimes when we practise loving-kindness we may experience feelings of warmth, happiness and kindness. If this is the case, then we can tune into these feelings, working with the principle of *'energy follows focus'*. By focusing on such experiences we nurture the habit of kindness, helping the brain to rewire itself, so that the habit flourishes.

Sometimes when we practise loving-kindness we encounter blocks and obstacles. We may even feel the very opposite of being loving and kind! We may feel resistance to the practice or we may feel ourselves shutting down. It is important not to get discouraged at this point, but to realise that this is a great opportunity to get to know our unique combination of blocks and obstacles. The practice is simply to become curious and notice the thoughts, emotions and physical sensations that arise when we feel blocked. We are not trying to control or fix the situation, but just be present. We can choose to rest with our Mindfulness support and simultaneously open up to our experience of the block or obstacle that has arisen. Recalling the principle *'the seeing is the doing'*, as we get to see it more clearly and impartially, its power over us will gradually diminish.

The obstacles we expose during loving-kindness practice can often be very painful. If we find that we become overwhelmed during the practice, we can simply reaffirm our intention to cultivate loving-kindness in the future and focus instead on basic Mindfulness practice.

Loving-kindness for Other

Follow the exercise written out below or follow the guided audio.

Do this exercise for around 20 minutes.

In the formal practice of loving-kindness, begin as you would with any of your Mindfulness practices: check in with your posture, reflect on your intention and motivation and then move through the normal stages of settling, grounding, resting and support.

Now bring to mind a dear friend or pet: some being in your life that you love dearly, but with whom you have a straightforward relationship. It may take a while for someone to come to mind and so be patient and allow your experience to unfold in its own way and in its own time. Imagine that they are sitting here in front of you. Notice what happens when you do this. Are there any thoughts, emotions or physical sensations that arise in your experience when you bring this dear friend to mind? Be curious about whatever happens. Stay grounded and in touch with physical sensations in the body.

Then after a while begin saying loving-kindness phrases for them:

- *May you be happy*
- *May you be healthy*
- *May you be safe*
- *May you live with ease*

If the phrases do not resonate with you, then make up some of your own. Notice what happens when you begin to say these loving-kindness phrases. Perhaps your heart opens and you feel sensations of warmth and kindness or perhaps your heart closes and you feel resistance or numbness. Simply notice whatever happens, with an attitude of openness and curiosity. Allow your experience of the practice to unfold on its own, without trying to make it turn out a particular way.

As you come to the end of the practice, notice what it feels like to broaden the circle of your awareness to include all of those with whom you share your day-to-day lives: your family, your neighbours, your colleagues, your friends, and your pets. Moreover, you can continue to expand your loving-kindness, in ever-widening circles, to include all living beings with whom you share the world.

As you come to the end of your practice time, let go of the loving-kindness practice and focus lightly on your support of breath or sound. Notice if there are any thoughts, emotions or sensations leftover from the practice and simply let them be.

Three Stage Breathing Space Revisited

Spend a few minutes reflecting back over your practice of the three stage breathing space from the last two weeks. Then answer the following questions:

How often are you doing the three stage breathing space?

_____

_____

_____

What helps you to remember to do the three stage breathing space?

_____

_____

_____

_____

Does it help you in your daily life to do the three stage breathing space, and if so how?

_____

_____

_____

What might help you to do the three stage breathing space more regularly (if applicable)?

_____

_____

_____

From now on, as well as doing the three stage breathing space at set times three times a day, begin to do the practice during moments of difficulty in your daily life and during moments of happiness in your daily life.

In a moment of difficulty or happiness you may have less time to do the practice, but now you are familiar with it you can do it quite quickly, if necessary. Simply check in with how you are: thoughts, emotions and sensations. Then take a few mindful breaths. Then spread out your focus from the breath to become aware of your whole experience, with a sense of allowing it to be as it is. In difficult situations it can be helpful to move to a different room, such as the bathroom, to do the practice in private, before moving mindfully on to the next moments of the day.

When you find yourself triggered in daily life situations and about to react angrily, simply remembering the three stage breathing space can often help you to respond in a more skilful way than usual.

Practice Schedule for the Week after Session Five

Formal Practice

Alternate the Noticing the Undercurrent Practice (you can use the guided audio from the webpage on page 6 or adapt the SGRS with breath or sound practice from the MBLC app) with the Loving-Kindness for Other Practice (you can use the guided audio from the MBLC app or on the webpage listed on page 6). At the end of each session, reflect on what happened during your period of practice and make notes below. Write down what you noticed arising within the undercurrent and your attitude towards what arose. Also, make notes of your attitude towards what happened when you did the Loving-Kindness Practice.

Day 1

_____

_____

_____

_____

Day 2

_____

_____

_____

_____

Day 3

_____

_____

_____

Day 4

_____

_____

_____

Day 5

_____

_____

_____

Day 6

_____

_____

_____

Day 7

_____

_____

_____

Informal Daily Life Practice

Continue with your previous daily life activities and again add another one. Write here what your new daily life activity is going to be:

Do the three stage breathing space three times a day, each day this week and at moments of difficulty and moments of happiness in your daily life.

Say loving-kindness phrases to yourself for people you pass in the street. You can smile at them as you say the phrases.

Describe below what you noticed when doing your informal daily life practice:

Day 1

Day 2

Day 3

Day 4

_____

_____

_____

Day 5

_____

_____

_____

Day 6

_____

_____

_____

Day 7

_____

_____

_____

Chapter 7

Session Six – Exploring the Attitude of the Observer

Reflecting on the Undercurrent

Set a timer for five minutes and then sit down and reflect back over your practice for the last week or so. How do you feel about the thoughts, emotions and feelings you have noticed in your practice? How do you feel about the mind being distracted? How do you feel about the mind being calm?

Now write down here what you noticed during your reflection:

_____

_____

_____

This reflection may show how we are constantly judging, evaluating and assessing the content of the undercurrent: the involuntary arising of thoughts, images and emotions. In all likelihood we want to have happy thoughts and for the mind to be calm and peaceful. We don't want to have unhappy thoughts and we don't want the mind to be distracted, agitated or bored. We attach a lot of importance to the undercurrent and believe that the content of the undercurrent is real and significant.

But as we discovered in the last chapter, the undercurrent is autonomous: it arises by itself and if we leave it alone it will liberate itself. It is an echo of the past that we cannot change by direct intervention. So most of the time our efforts to manipulate and control it are a complete waste of time. Once we have seen this clearly, we shift the focus of our practice to the *attitude* with which we observe the undercurrent. In other words, we shift our focus to the observer. This is the part of the mind that can be trained, and this is where real change can occur. At this point it might be useful to introduce a metaphor to get a sense of how we view the observer and begin to train it.

Sitting on a Riverbank

The Observer and Undercurrent model is well illustrated by the metaphor of sitting on a riverbank and watching the river flow by. The observer is part of us sitting on the riverbank and the undercurrent is the river. We train the observer to sit on the bank and simply be aware of this thought-stream, noticing and accepting whatever floats by, but hopefully not sliding down the bank and into the river itself; not becoming involved with the content of our thoughts. This is the heart of Mindfulness practice.

But how often do we just sit and watch the river flow by?

Most of the time we find ourselves floating downstream before we even realise we have slid off the bank. This is a metaphor for engaging with a thought that arises in the mind and getting caught up in thinking. Once we are in the river we are caught in the flow of the undercurrent, immersed in distraction, very soon to be buffeted by the waves and dragged under the water. The undercurrent can take us anywhere: we might be carried into clear pools with beautiful fish and the very next moment thrown headlong over a turbulent waterfall, and then marooned in a murky backwater. Where we go depends upon the force of the habitual tendencies which have been triggered within us.

Through Mindfulness practice we notice how we have been caught in the undercurrent and dragged along. We become acquainted with the power of distraction. At this point we have a choice: to continue to be dragged along by the river, or to climb back on to the riverbank. Becoming aware of this choice and learning to exercise it is the birth of freedom. So we might well choose to sit back on the bank and impartially watch the river flow by, until a powerful movement within the river draws us back into the water – and so it goes on! This is the nature of Mindfulness practice. This is how awareness grows and wisdom is born – through falling back into the river and climbing back on to the riverbank again and again.

In this way we begin to see that through our practice so far we have been training the observer – training to sit on the riverbank and to focus on a Mindfulness support, while at the same time being aware of how the river flows by; to recognise when we fall into the river and become caught in the undercurrent; and finally to climb out of the river and to sit once more on the riverbank.

More importantly we have been training the observer to be OK about this whole process; to be allowing, kind and curious about falling in and climbing out; to accept this process and appreciate that nothing is wrong.

Thus far in our training we have been paying attention to the undercurrent and how the observer engages with the undercurrent. Now we turn our attention to the observer itself and learn to observe the observer. This involves a 180-degree shift in focus and it brings us to the next exercise.

Noticing Attitude

Follow the exercise written out below or follow the guided audio.

Do this exercise for about 20 minutes.

Start with an intention to stay present and notice the attitude of the observer. Then spend a few moments reflecting on your motivation for doing this. Then move on to settling, grounding, resting, and either breath or sound support.

Now focus on your Mindfulness support in a very relaxed way and be careful not to obstruct thoughts. In fact, develop an interest in the fact that thoughts keep arising in your mind. Learn to watch them so that gradually the existence of the undercurrent becomes clear to you. Each time you notice that you have become caught up in thinking, notice where the mind has wandered to and then kindly but firmly bring your attention back to the Mindfulness support.

Once you are settled again on the support notice the arising of thoughts within the mind and gently inquire how you feel about how you are feeling right now – physically, mentally or emotionally. Maybe you are agitated or tense, maybe lots of thoughts are spinning through your mind, perhaps you are feeling light and open, or maybe low or despondent – how do you feel about this? Do you have an expectation that Mindfulness practice should make you feel in a particular way? If you don't feel the way you want, what is your reaction to this?

As you come to the end of your session rest without any focus for a while and let go of the effort to 'meditate'. Then finish your session and make some notes in your journal of what came up for you when you inquired into the attitude of your observer.

This exercise will familiarise us with the attitude our observer has towards what is arising in the undercurrent. For many of us it is very common to have a judgmental or critical attitude to what arises in our experience. Noticing this is an important first step. We are then in a position to work with this attitude and to begin to cultivate an attitude of allowing and acceptance. This will be the focus of the next chapter.

Before we begin to train the observer, however, we need to address an important question that comes out of the last exercise: why can we not leave the undercurrent alone? When we explored the undercurrent in the last chapter, it became clear that it is an echo of the past, and if we leave it alone it will arise by itself, display itself and liberate itself. But how often do we find ourselves doing this? And why is this so hard to do? These questions go to the root of the inquiry we have engaged in with the observer and undercurrent model.

What becomes clear when we pay attention to the observer is that it observes with *preference*. In other words, we have strong habits of like and dislike when it comes to our inner world –

and indeed the outer world. If unpleasant feelings arise there is a movement in the mind towards avoidance, pushing away and trying to manipulate or change the feelings. Whereas if pleasant feelings arise there is a movement towards prolonging or holding on to the feelings. We all know how it feels to have a 'good practice session' when we feel spacious, open and at peace. At a subtle level we tend to try to prolong this experience; and if anxious feelings arise there is a subtle, barely seen movement of the mind to avoid and suppress. This is what we mean by preference, and this is thrown up by the inquiry we just did in the last exercise of 'how do you feel about what you feel'.

When we pay attention to our preferences what we then see is that there is a sense of 'me' that lies behind these preferences – like an unseen puppeteer moving the puppets in different ways. We see that this sense of self resides in the observer and it has a strong vested interest in what arises within our mind. It is as if this sense of self says: "This is me, I am here, I am thinking..." This sense of self is ruled by preference: "Is this a nice thought that has popped up? Do I like the emotion that has arisen? Does this mind state make me feel good? ..." We all have similar voices running through our minds. Furthermore, when we move about our daily lives this inner voice is always active, checking whether external reality meets our preferences: "Do I like this restaurant, does this menu have what I need? And do I like the people sitting around me at the tables..." It is as if we are constantly scanning our inner and outer worlds to see if reality meets with our preferences.

Rob Nairn has coined a wonderful term for this sense of self that resides in the observer. He calls it the "egocentric preference system", generally known by the catchy acronym: EPS. Each of us has a unique EPS lodged within the observer. We explore the workings of the EPS in more detail when we do the Insight Training offered by the Mindfulness Association. At this stage the main thing to notice is that there is a sense of self embedded in the observer. Seldom do we observe in a neutral way. We observe with preference ruled by a strong sense of self. Simply acknowledging this fact is a big step in Mindfulness training, because we come face-to-face with the main architect of our suffering, and in so doing we have the opportunity to cultivate a different kind of observer: one that is more compassionate and accepting. This is a key theme of the Compassion Training offered by the Mindfulness Association.

The EPS is the main architect of our suffering because it insists of doing the impossible: fixing, sanitising, manipulating or changing the undercurrent. So many people walk around immersed in the undercurrent, with an overactive EPS that is constantly trying to do something about it! Difficult feelings or issues arise and then we dwell on them and unwittingly try to twist them into a different set of feelings or squeeze out some resolution – none of which works. In fact all that happens is that the undercurrent gets more churned up, we get battered about on its inner reefs, and the EPS gets into a frenzy of agitation trying to do the impossible! This might sound funny, but it is very painful and describes the inner reality of so many people.

When we see clearly that the undercurrent is simply an echo of the past that arises by itself and liberates itself, and when we see clearly that the EPS is a victim of its own preferences, we can then gradually begin to separate out these two processes within the mind. Simply put, this involves noticing what arises in the undercurrent, noticing the preferences that arise in reaction to this, and beginning to accept both and not feed either. This is the key to freedom.

Being Kind to Ourselves

This practice builds on that in the last chapter, where we cultivated loving-kindness for a person or animal for whom we felt a natural flow of affection, by bringing them to mind and saying these loving-kindness phrases for them:

- May you be happy
- May you be healthy
- May you be safe
- May you live with ease

In this practice we recognise that just as our dear friend or pet wishes to be happy and to experience well-being, so too we wish to be happy and to experience well-being. So we begin to say these phrases for ourselves. This might not be so easy at first because many of us have an ingrained habit of being hard on ourselves or thinking that we are not worthy of kindness or thinking that if we are kind to ourselves we might lose our drive to succeed. But let's take a moment to revisit our working definition of loving-kindness:

The genuine wish for the happiness and well-being of ourselves and others.

How can it be wrong to wish that we be happy? How can it be wrong to wish that we experience well-being? These are interesting questions to reflect upon, especially if we find ourselves struggling to be kind to ourselves.

It is important to distinguish between self-kindness and self-indulgence. While it might be kind to have one glass of wine when we get home from work in order to relax, it would be self-indulgent to finish the whole bottle! Similarly, it might be kind to ourselves to leave the washing up one day, because we have had a very busy time at work, but it would be self-indulgent to do this every day, especially if this means that our partner has to do it all the time. So we need to reflect on the long-term implications of our behaviour to determine whether it is self-kindness or self-indulgence. The key questions are: "What do I really need?" as opposed to "What do I want?" "Will my actions lead to my well-being and the well-being of others in the long term?" Then we simply follow our own wisdom on the matter, without giving ourselves a hard time.

There may be many blocks to being kind to ourselves, but the first step is to develop an intention to be kind. An example of such an intention is: "*I would like to be more kind to myself and to take better care of myself.*" Then we can develop our motivation: Why do we want to be more kind to ourselves? Perhaps if we are more kind to ourselves we will feel more at ease and be happier. Then we can recognise that this will not just benefit us, but also those around us. Most of us tend to be more grumpy and reactive when we are unhappy and this leads us to be more selfish and less generous to those around us. Being unhappy can make us angry and frustrated and say things that we regret later. We can see in others too how bad behaviour mostly arises out of unhappiness. So developing kindness to ourselves is not selfish. On the contrary, it is the best way we can become more kind to others.

The Dalai Lama often says, "*My religion is kindness,*" and he is an example of a very happy man, despite the great difficulties he has faced in his life.

When we practise loving-kindness towards ourselves, we are not trying to force anything or squeeze out any particular feeling from our hearts. If things feel dry or distant, that is fine. That is our experience. We can allow whatever is there just to be there as it is. As we said above, the first step is forming the intention to be kind. This plants the seeds of kindness that may take some time to mature into actual feelings of kindness. So being patient with ourselves is important too.

We might find that during this practice our hearts open and we experience feelings of warmth and connection. So from time-to-time during the practice we can move our awareness into our body to sense how kindness feels in the body. Alternatively, we might find that blocks to kindness, such as fear, anxiety or anger, arise. This is completely fine and it does not mean that our practice has gone wrong. It provides us with an opportunity to learn more about ourselves and about our habitual patterns of contraction and shutting down. If this happens, we can move our awareness into our body to sense how the block feels in our body. As Pema Chodron often says, if we do loving-kindness practice and feelings of love and warmth flow that is very good, but if instead we feel blocks to kindness and go numb that is very good too, because we are learning about ourselves. The key point here is that whatever happens is part of the practice and part of our own unique process of growth and unfolding.

Since many of us struggle with saying the loving-kindness phrases to ourselves as we are, here are some alternatives:

Firstly, we can recognise that just as our dear friend wishes to have happiness and well-being, so do we, and that there is nothing wrong with that. Then we can imagine ourselves sitting with our dear friend, perhaps holding hands or imagining some other gesture of connection between ourselves and our friend. Then we can say these phrases for both ourselves and our dear friend:

- May we be happy
- May we be healthy
- May we be safe
- May we live with ease

We can notice how this feels and if it feels OK we can then say the phrases for ourselves as we are now. If that is difficult then go back to saying the phrases once again for ourselves and our dear friend.

A second alternative is to imagine a younger version of ourselves such as when we were a child. Then we can say the loving-kindness phrases for our younger self, perhaps using our name in the phrases. Again, notice how this feels and if it feels OK we can then say the phrases for ourselves as we are now. If that is difficult then go back to saying the phrases once again for our younger self.

While doing this practice it may happen that we say the phrases as a way of blocking out our present moment experience, in particular uncomfortable feelings. If this happens we can once again bring our awareness into the body and notice what sensations are present. This will help us stay in touch with our present moment experience.

It is always useful to remember the key Mindfulness principle of 'energy follows focus' when we do loving-kindness practice. If feelings of warmth and kindness arise take some time to savour them and they will grow. If feelings of fear or anger arise simply notice how these feel in the body without getting caught up in the storyline. If we get involved in the thoughts that spring out of fear or anger we feed more energy into the habits of fear or anger.

Sometimes there is an element of 'faking it until you make it' with loving-kindness practice. If the practice feels a bit artificial to start with, see this as part of the process and just keep going. If we have formed a strong intention and motivation then at some point the practice will come alive and the feelings will start to flow.

Loving-kindness for Self and Other

Follow the exercise written out below or follow the guided audio.

Do this exercise for about 20 minutes.

In the formal practice of loving-kindness, you begin as you would with any of your Mindfulness practices: adopt your sitting posture, reflect on intention and motivation and then practise settling, grounding and resting in the normal way, using a Mindfulness support of breath or sound to stay present when your mind wanders. Now bring to mind a dear friend (or animal): someone in your life whom you love dearly but with whom you have a straightforward relationship. It may take a while for someone to come to mind and so be patient and allow your experience to unfold in its own way and in its own time. Imagine that this person or animal is sitting in front of you. Notice what happens when you do this. Are there any thoughts, emotions or physical sensations that arise when you bring this dear friend or animal to mind? Be curious about whatever happens. Stay grounded and in touch with physical sensations in your body.

Then begin to say loving-kindness phrases for this dear friend or animal:

- *May you be happy*
- *May you be healthy*
- *May you be safe*
- *May you live with ease*

Notice what happens when you say the loving-kindness phrases for the dear friend or animal. Perhaps your heart opens and you feel sensations of warmth and kindness, or maybe your heart closes and you feel resistance or numbness. Simply notice and be open to whatever happens, with an attitude of curiosity. Allow your experience of the practice to unfold in its own way, without interfering or trying to make the practice turn out a particular way.

Now reflect for a moment that just as your dear friend or animal wishes to be happy and to experience well-being so do you wish to be happy and experience well-being. Bring to mind your intention to be kind to yourself and your motivation for doing so. Then begin saying the phrases for yourself:

- *May I be happy*
- *May I be healthy*
- *May I be safe*
- *May I live with ease*

Experiment with alternating 'I' in the phrases above with saying your name. If the practice is difficult, then try saying the phrases for yourself and your dear friend together or for a younger version of yourself, as described above.

Notice what happens when you begin to say the phrases for yourself. Does your heart open or do you feel resistance or numbness? Simply notice and be open to whatever happens, with an attitude of curiosity. Allow your experience of the practice to unfold in its own way. There is no right or wrong way for your experience to be.

Now notice what it feels like to broaden the circle of your loving-kindness to include all of those with whom you share your daily life: your family, your neighbours, your colleagues, your friends, and your pets. Moreover, you can continue to expand your loving-kindness, in ever-widening circles, to include all those with whom you share the world.

As you come to the end of your practice session, let go of the loving-kindness practice and simply rest with your Mindfulness support of breath or of sound. Notice if there are any thoughts, emotions or sensations leftover from the practice.

Practice Schedule for the Week after Session Six

Formal Practice

Alternate doing the Noticing the Attitude of the Observer practice (you can use the Noticing Attitude guided audio from the webpage listed on page 6 or adapt the SGRS with breath or sound from the MBLC app) with the Loving-kindness for Self and Other practice (you can use the guided audio from the MBLC app or on the webpage listed on page 6). At the end of the practice, reflect on what happened during your period of practice and make notes below. In particular, write down what you noticed about your attitude towards what arose within the undercurrent. Also, make notes of your attitude towards what happened when you did the loving-kindness practice. See if you can identify any attitudes, preferences, assumptions, expectations and goals.

Day 1

_____

_____

_____

Day 2

_____

_____

_____

Day 3

_____

_____

_____

Day 4

_____

_____

_____

Day 5

_____

_____

_____

Day 6

_____

_____

_____

Day 7

_____

_____

_____

Informal Daily Life Practice

Continue with your previous daily life activities and again add another one. Write here what your new daily life activity is going to be:

_____

_____

Continue to do the three stage breathing space three times a day, each day this week and at moments of difficulty and moments of happiness in your daily life. At the end of the three stage breathing space, say some loving-kindness phrases to yourself. Try smiling to yourself as you say the phrases.

Describe below what you noticed when you did your informal daily life practice:

Day 1

_____

_____

_____

Day 2

_____

_____

_____

Day 3

_____

_____

_____

Day 4

_____

_____

_____

Day 5

_____

_____

_____

Day 6

_____

_____

_____

Day 7

_____

_____

_____

Chapter 8

Session Seven – Acceptance & Self-Compassion

Acceptance

Let's revisit our definition of Mindfulness:

Knowing what is happening, while it is happening, without preference.

Throughout this workbook we have been exploring two key elements of Mindfulness training: method and attitude. The method is "knowing what is happening while it is happening..." and it provides a technique for working with a Mindfulness support. The attitude is one of "... without preference" and it explains how we approach the technique. If we use the basic method in a harsh and impersonal way – impatient with ourselves and critical of the thoughts that arise in our minds – then Mindfulness will not produce any meaningful change. In fact it might even strengthen the power of the self-critic, who then has another stick to beat us with, namely the Mindfulness support! So attitude is crucial.

There are two main elements to this attitude: acceptance and kindness. Acceptance is cultivating an inner attitude of allowing and non-struggle with what arises within our experience. Kindness is bringing a quality of warmth and friendliness both to ourselves and to what we experience. Building on the work we have already done practising kindness to self and others in the previous chapters, we will now look more closely at acceptance and then self-compassion. Chris Germer (2009) makes a useful distinction between the two, by saying that acceptance relates to our attitude towards our inner experience of difficult feelings and emotions, whilst self-compassion relates to the *person* who has the experience. It is generally easier first to accept our experience and then afterwards to bring acceptance and kindness to the person 'in here' having the experience.

People often misunderstand the meaning of acceptance in the context of Mindfulness training. This is partly to do with how the English word 'acceptance' is commonly understood. So the first step is to clear up any misconceptions. To accept something does not mean that we have to condone or approve it, and nor does it mean that we have to like it. It does not mean that we have to resign ourselves passively to an unpleasant situation that will not change. Simply put, it means that we clearly come to terms with what is actually going on in our experience, without wasting time and energy in fighting with what is going on. It means turning towards and welcoming whatever has arisen in our experience. This enables us to see the full picture with clarity and without bias. We are then in a position to know what course of action to take, if indeed any action is required. On the contrary, if we fight with difficult emotions and feelings, then we have two problems: the difficult feeling itself *and* our dislike of and resistance to it. This makes it especially difficult to know how to respond to the situation, because our inner judgment is under the power of our resistance. In all likelihood our response will not be a skilful one, but one of habitual reaction.

For example, while we are practising we notice an inner movement of anxiety and a dropping of our mood. If we instinctively react to this and brace against it, then it is hard to relate skilfully to what is arising, and most likely we will get carried away by our resistance. This might even involve tightening around the Mindfulness support and suppressing the feelings. The outcome will be tension and loss of awareness as our mind contracts against the feelings. On the contrary, if we notice the feelings and simply allow them to be present, while at the same time focusing lightly on the Mindfulness support, we are in a position to open up to the feelings and discern what we need. When we finish the session this might mean taking a bit of time out in the day to go for a walk, or simply slowing down or doing less that day. So acceptance is a form of clear discernment that lays the ground for wise action.

Two Arrows Sutra

There is a lovely teaching (or 'Sutra') of the Buddha that clearly illustrates the importance of acceptance. It is called the "Sutra of the Arrows" and it relates how even the good and the wise are regularly struck by the first arrow, which is that of the unavoidable pain of life. All of us – even saints – have to experience the pain of illness, loss, disappointments, ups and downs, aging and death. Most of us, however, are struck by a second arrow, which is more painful than the first, because it lands in the area of the body that is already inflamed by the wound of the first arrow. This is the arrow of 'resistance obsession': not wanting to feel the pain of the first arrow. So many of us put a huge amount of energy into resisting, avoiding, suppressing or dissociating from the first arrow, because we do not want to feel the pain. The wise ones realise that this simply does not work, but the rest of us are so caught up in our habitual preferences that we feel not only the pain of the first arrow, but also the suffering inflicted by the second. According to Rob Nairn (MA lecture 2008), the first arrow is 10% and the second arrow 90% of the problem.

As Clive Holmes (MA lecture 2009) aptly pointed out, in modern times many of us are struck by a third arrow (not part of the original Sutra), which can become a fatal blow to our sense of self-worth. This is the arrow of thinking that something is wrong with us, because we have been struck by two arrows. This is the arrow of shame, which is a great scourge in the West. In the words of Paul Gilbert:

Shame is that self we do not want to feel and do not want to be in touch with. It comes with a feeling that there is something not quite right, or indeed very wrong with us; that if people knew what was going on in our minds they would not like us very much and might even be repelled by us... The problem with shame is that not only does it put us into hiding from others, but also from ourselves.

Gilbert and Choden (2013, pp 193–196)

The remedy to the first two arrows is acceptance. By learning to face the reality of our experience, we allow ourselves to feel the pain of the first arrow. The antidote to the second arrow of 'resistance obsession' comes from accepting and seeing clearly the painful and difficult feelings, emotions and mind states that arise within us. Self-compassion is the antidote to the feelings of unworthiness and shame caused by the third arrow. It brings kindness and support to the person 'in here' who is struggling to cope with the first two arrows.

Something important to bear in mind with acceptance is that we are discussing it in relation to the internal environment of the mind, with its involuntary arising of thoughts, emotions and sensations. We are not talking about acceptance of outer events and situations; although if we cultivate acceptance of what arises within our inner world, this will inform how we relate to the external world. The important point here is that different rules apply to the inner and the outer world. At the level of the outer world we might well need to stand up to things and be proactive. Many people think that acceptance means being apathetic in the face of social injustice and doing nothing. This is a big misconception. When we speak about acceptance in the context of Mindfulness, we are referring to the inner level of how we relate to what arises within the mind. Here it might be more skilful to do nothing, be the impartial witness of what arises and make space for our thoughts and feelings to unfold in their own way. In this case all we need to know about an issue or an experience will be revealed, by giving our thoughts and feelings space to play themselves out. We don't have to do anything. Trying to resolve and understand an issue tends to get us stuck in dwelling, ruminating and picking at our thoughts and feelings. This is counterproductive, because it involves compulsive thinking activity, which is precisely what created our problems in the first place.

As Rob Nairn likes to say (MA lecture, 2009):

Little Bo Peep has lost her sheep and doesn't know where to find them, but just leave them alone and they will come home, bringing their TALES (not tails!) behind them.

In this analogy, the sheep are our thoughts and if we leave them alone they will tell us their tales; that is they will reveal what we need to know about them, or the underlying issues that lie beneath them. They only do this, however, if we leave them alone and this involves unconditional acceptance of whatever is arising within the mind.

Practising Acceptance: RAIN method

There is a very accessible method for practising acceptance that goes by the acronym RAIN. RAIN is a way of approaching, befriending and making space for difficult emotions or mind states that arise within us. However, as psychologist Paul Gilbert has pointed out, many people have trouble accepting positive emotions, so RAIN can apply equally to negative and positive emotions, mind states and any thought patterns that we have trouble 'letting in'. The four stages of RAIN are as follows:

Recognise – noticing what arises within the mind;
Allow – allowing what arises within the mind to do so on its
    own terms, without engaging or interfering with it;
Intimate Attention – paying close attention to thoughts,

emotions and mind states, particularly those which recur; Non-identification – making space for these thoughts, emotions and mind states to move through us, recognising that they are changing all the time and do not define who we are.

To assist our understanding of the RAIN method of acceptance, we can think of our mind like a guesthouse, with the guests that come and go being like the different thoughts, emotions and mind states that move through us.

"The Guest House" by Rumi

This being human is a guesthouse
Every morning a new arrival
A joy, a depression, a meanness,
some momentary awareness comes
as an unexpected visitor.
Welcome and entertain them all!
Even if they are a crowd of sorrows,
Who violently sweep your house
empty of its furniture,
still, treat each guest honourably.
He may be clearing you out
for some new delight.
The dark thought, the shame, the malice,
meet them at the door laughing,
and invite them in.
Be grateful for whoever comes,
because each has been sent
as a guide from beyond.

To begin with the RAIN exercise can seem quite complicated, but if we reflect back we might recall how the settling, grounding, resting and support (SGRS) routine seemed complicated at first.

Once we become familiar with RAIN, we will see how one stage flows naturally into the next, just like the stages of SGRS flowed naturally from one to another.

It can also help to understand that we are already very familiar with the first two stages of RAIN, which are *'recognising'* and *'allowing'*. These are part of our normal Mindfulness practice. As we rest with our Mindfulness support, we are practising *'knowing what is happening while it is happening'*, which is the *'recognising'* stage of the RAIN practice. This is like opening the door and acknowledging the guest who wants to come into our internal guesthouse.

We have also been practising *'without preference'*, which is the *'allowing'* stage of the RAIN practice. We simply allow whatever is arising within the mind to be present. This is like welcoming the guest and inviting it to take a seat inside our internal guesthouse.

The second two stages of *'intimate attention'* and *'non-identification'* are especially useful when strong mind states or emotions arise that strongly draw our attention. Rob Nairn calls this the *'elastic band syndrome'*, because it is like our attention is repeatedly drawn to these issues as if connected to them by an elastic band. When we notice this happening during our practice we introduce the other two steps of RAIN.

'Intimate attention' is like getting to know the guest in our guesthouse. We practise it in four stages:

Mindfulness of body

Firstly we bring our attention to where the difficulty is held within our body. Then we notice what kind of sensations we are experiencing in this part of the body – maybe there is a tightness, contraction, heat, vibration... – and whether we are resisting these sensations. Finally we notice what happens if we open to them with Mindfulness and acceptance.

Mindfulness of feelings

Then we bring our attention to the emotions and feelings connected with the experience. We notice what the tone of primary feeling is and then observe what layers of feeling make up the experience. We may notice that the presenting emotion is not just one feeling, but a constellation of feelings. We try to meet each of these feelings with Mindfulness and acceptance.

Mindfulness of thoughts

Next, we notice what kind of thoughts, stories or beliefs are spinning around the experience. We try to take a step back and look at these thoughts: Are they true or one sided? Are they permanent or changing moment-by-moment? Do the stories we tell ourselves about this experience make it seem more solid, real and permanent?

Mindfulness of underlying processes

Then we notice how we are relating to our experience. Are we taking the emotion or mind state to be solid and real? Are we seeing it as permanent? Are we clinging to it and contracting around it? Finally, are we identifying with it as who we are in this moment?

'Mindfulness of underlying processes' leads to the final stage of RAIN, which is 'non-identification'. Here we enquire of every mental state or emotion that arises: is this really who I am or is this just an experience that is moving through me? Through practising in this way we may come to see that the presenting emotion or difficulty is not who we are – it is simply a guest moving through our internal guesthouse of awareness.

To familiarise ourselves with the process we can bring to mind a persistent issue or difficult experience in our lives, and then work with it through the different stages of RAIN. Then, once we know the RAIN exercise well, we can do it whenever a difficulty arises in our practice or in our lives. To begin with it is best not to choose an issue that is too difficult, or stay focused on the difficulty for more than 5 minutes, as we may inadvertently start feeding energy into it. Instead, after paying *'intimate attention'* for a short while, we can move on to the *'non-identification'* stage and stay there for a while, as it will help to develop a healthy perspective in relation to the issue.

It might be useful to give an everyday example to bring the RAIN process to life. Imagine that we are sitting one morning doing our daily practice and things feel pretty good. The mind is still, we feel energised and spacious, and there is a feeling of enthusiasm for the day ahead. Even though we know that we are not supposed to become attached to 'good experiences', we hope to prolong these feelings, because we know that we have a busy day ahead, and we need all the clarity and head space we can muster. Just then there is a movement of emotion within us that feels unwelcome. A cloud of anxiety and threatening low mood threatens to disrupt our clear blue sky. At this point there might be a subtle movement to suppress these emotions, by closing in tightly around the Mindfulness support as we pretend not to hear the knock of Anxiety on the door of our internal guesthouse. This will not work in the long run because our mind will contract and our treasured spaciousness and calm will be lost.

So this is where we practise RAIN. The first step is simply to acknowledge the feeling of anxiety and name it. It is like we go to the door of the guesthouse and open it, and say, "Anxiety, hello!" The second stage of RAIN is to welcome Anxiety into our guesthouse. In fact, anxiety is already in, so the second stage is a way of not fighting with what is already happening. Also, we might notice that there are other guests queuing up behind Anxiety. There might be Low Mood and also Resistance to both Anxiety and Low Mood. So we might say, "Anxiety, Low Mood and Resistance, please come in and have a cup of tea, make yourself at home!"

Now the first two stages of RAIN might be enough. This corresponds to the normal Mindfulness practice approach, which we discussed above. But in this case our friend Anxiety is pretty persistent and comes over to where we are meditating, leaving Low Mood to sulk over his cup of tea, while Resistance stares blankly at the wall ahead! Anxiety comes and sits next to us and starts breathing in a panicky way. Again, we might use the Mindfulness practice as a form of subtle suppression and note, "Anxiety breathing heavily," and come back to the support, with a feeling of annoyance that Anxiety and his entourage have not drunk up and left.

This is where we bring in the third stage of RAIN: we notice where we are holding the feelings of anxiety, low mood and resistance in our body; we notice how they feel, and what thoughts are moving through us; and we notice too how we are relating to these thoughts and feelings. In this way we give Anxiety intimate attention, without getting lost in the thoughts and stories that might spring from this mind state. Once we have paid close attention, we come back to the broader space of awareness – aware of the Mindfulness support, aware of our body and aware of the space around our experience. This is the stage of *'non-identification'*. In this way we acknowledge that Anxiety is simply a guest moving through us; it does not need to define or limit us. Ironically when we resist feelings we end up *becoming* them, and when we welcome and befriend them, they are free to move through us. This is the underlying wisdom of RAIN.

With this understanding, let's try doing the practice:

RAIN Exercise

Follow the exercise written out below or follow the guided audio.

Do this exercise for around 20 minutes.

To begin read "The Guesthouse" poem and then follow the normal routine of intention, motivation, settling, grounding, resting and

Mindfulness support using either sound or breath as the support.

Recognise:
When a difficult thought or emotion persistently knocks on the door of your internal guesthouse then engage with the RAIN exercise. Recognise what the presenting emotion is and name it. It is like opening the door and acknowledging the guest that wants to come in.

Allow:
Now open up to the emotion and allow it to be present. This is like welcoming the guest and inviting it to take a seat inside your guesthouse.

Then go back to the Mindfulness support but know that the guest is present within your guesthouse. If you find that the guest persistently calls for your attention then switch your focus to the presenting emotion and make it the focus of your Mindfulness practice. But do this in a particular way.

Intimate Attention (for about 5 minutes):
First bring your attention to where the emotion or difficulty is held within the body. Notice what kind of sensations you are experiencing in this part of the body – maybe there is a tightness, contraction, heat, vibration... etc. Notice if you are resisting these sensations. Then notice what happens if you open to them with Mindfulness and acceptance.

Now bring your attention to the emotions and feelings connected with the experience. Tune into what the primary feeling tone is and then observe what layers of feeling make up the experience. So you may notice that the presenting emotion is not one feeling, but a constellation of feelings. Then try to meet each of these feelings with Mindfulness and acceptance.

Next, notice what kind of thoughts or beliefs are spinning around the presenting emotion. Try to take a step back and look at these thoughts. Are they true or one sided? Are they permanent or changing moment-by-moment?

Finally, notice how you are relating to this experience. Are you taking the emotion to be solid and real? Are you seeing it as permanent? Are you clinging to it and contracting around it? Finally, are you identifying with it as who you are in this moment?

Non-identification:
This leads to the last stage of RAIN in which you inquire of every mind state or emotion that arises – is this really who I am or is this just an experience that is moving through me? Has it become who I am in this moment?

Through practising in this way you may come to see that the presenting emotion or difficulty is not who you are – it is just a guest moving through your guesthouse.

Self-Compassion

Having worked with the RAIN practice, we are now in a position to approach self-compassion. Integrating compassion into Mindfulness practice is a key element of this training. As our Mindfulness practice deepens there are many things we see in the mind that we may not like, such as challenging emotions like anger, lust, jealousy, sadness, amongst others. Perhaps we begin to see quite clearly that sometimes we can be cruel or selfish. When this happens we may have a habit of criticising ourselves and beating ourselves up for not being as we would ideally like to be. The problem is that this causes us to suffer even more. It is the second arrow we described above.

At this point it is useful to remember that our thinking and behaviour is habitual – it is the result of our past conditioning that we did not choose. There is no need therefore to blame ourselves when we see our flaws and our weaknesses. However, we can begin to take responsibility for how we think and behave in the future, by putting less energy into beating ourselves up and more energy into cultivating a kind and compassionate attitude to ourselves and others.

For this reason practising compassion is crucial because it generates an atmosphere within the mind that can help us to accept ourselves, just as we are, and on this basis begin to accept other people just as they are. This is the basis for genuine self-transformation and bringing healing to the network of relationships that make up our lives.

A useful analogy for practising Mindfulness is gradually turning up a dimmer switch that begins to reveal more and more of what is present in the mind, which at first is like a darkly-lit room. As our awareness strengthens the light begins to reveal dusty, broken furniture and strange objects in the shadows of the room, hitherto unseen. There is always the danger with Mindfulness that the more we see, the more we might begin to dislike what we see in the room and the self-critic can have a field day berating us for the junk piled up in the corners. Compassion is very important here, because it infuses a quality of warmth to the light as we turn up the dimmer switch. It is not a cold, neon light, but a warm, inclusive light.

So far in this training we have been practising kindness to self and others. This derives from the Buddhist practice of *maitri* or loving kindness that involves cultivating an attitude of friendliness to what we experience both in our mind and in the outer world. When *maitri* encounters suffering it becomes compassion. This is beautifully illustrated in the following quote:

When the sunlight of loving-kindness shines on the tears of suffering, the rainbow of compassion emerges.

Compassion can be defined as:

Sensitivity to the suffering of self and others, with a deep desire to relieve that suffering and its causes.
HH Dalai Lama

From this definition we can see that there are two aspects to compassion practice. Paul Gilbert refers to them as the "two psychologies of compassion" (*Mindful Compassion*, Gilbert and Choden, 2013). The first is turning to face the pain and difficulty we experience, which we have been training to do as part of our Mindfulness practice. The second is building up an inner resource from which to respond to and alleviate suffering.

At this stage of our training the main focus is self-compassion – being willing to face our own pain and suffering, and responding to it with kindness and understanding. The reason for the focus on self-compassion is twofold. Firstly, many of us are naturally compassionate to others, but often do not extend compassion to ourselves. Think about how critical we are to ourselves, and how we beat ourselves up for the smallest slip-up. If someone else was that critical about us we might well have nothing to do with them, and yet we let the self-critic belittle and attack us day in and day out! Secondly, when we become more compassionate towards ourselves, and our own suffering, there is an accompanying growth of our compassion towards others. When we see clearly how we cause ourselves to suffer there is a natural movement of empathy and understanding for others who struggle in the same way.

American psychologist and researcher Kristin Neff has developed a model of self-compassion which, as described in her book *Self-Compassion*, involves three elements:

- Extending kindness and understanding to ourselves, rather than harsh self-judgment;
- Seeing our own experience of suffering as part of the larger human experience, rather than separating and isolating ourselves;
- Holding our own painful thoughts and feelings in balanced awareness, rather than over-identifying with them.

Typically, when we experience a difficulty in life, we tend to judge ourselves and think that there is something wrong with us. Often, we think that we are the only person in the world who is so useless – we may become ashamed of our difficulty and so we hide it from others. In this way we isolate ourselves in our difficulty and separate ourselves from others. We feel that this difficulty is too big to endure, and yet by focusing on it all the time, it ends up defining who we are. This only increases our suffering and is the third arrow we described above.

If we apply self-compassion when we are in difficulty, we acknowledge that there is nothing wrong with us; it is simply an experience we are going through. RAIN practice helps us to see this and realise that it makes sense to look after ourselves in a kind and caring way when we experience a difficulty. We understand that every human being's life can throw up many difficulties and that we are not perfect and that is OK. We also recognise that the human condition is not one of perfection. We all make mistakes and that is OK too. Any challenging emotion we are feeling, such as anger, sadness, shame or grief, is also being experienced by countless human beings around the planet. These emotions have been experienced by human beings since we first evolved. In this way we are not alone in our suffering; we don't have to be ashamed of our difficulties, because everyone experiences difficulties some of the time. Also, we can bring mindful awareness to our difficult feelings, allowing them to move through us in their own way, rather than endlessly thinking about them and elaborating on them until they completely overwhelm us!

Self-Compassion Break

This is a daily-life practice developed by Kristin Neff and is based on the model described above. Do this short practice whenever you experience a difficulty in your daily life.

Follow the exercise written out below or follow the guided audio from the MBLC app.

Do this exercise for around 3 minutes.

Make a gesture of self-soothing, such as placing your hand(s) on your heart, hugging yourself or holding your own hand.

Breathe deeply in and out.

Speak kindly to yourself, really letting yourself experience what is behind the words, and spending some time with each of the phrases:

~ *This is a moment of suffering (or difficulty).*
~ *Suffering is part of everyone's life.*
~ *May I be kind to myself in this moment.*

Three Emotional Systems

This model of three emotional systems has been developed by Professor Paul Gilbert and is derived from neuroscience research. It is explained in more detail in the book *Mindful Compassion* (2013) written by Professor Gilbert and Choden. The reason for including it in this chapter is to get a broader understanding of how our emotions work and to understand where we need to focus in order to cultivate self-compassion.

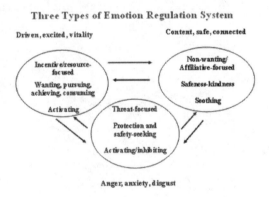

From Gilbert (2009) *Compassionate Mind*

The model describes how the evolved brain has three emotional systems:

- A threat and self-protection system;
- A drive and resource seeking system; and
- A soothing and contentment system.

The threat system is always on the lookout for threats to our safety and to the safety of our loved ones. It is connected with the emotions of anger, anxiety and disgust, which arise when we experience a threat. It is also associated with the behaviours of fight, flight, freeze or submit, which are the types of behaviour we exhibit in the face of a threat. Some of us are more likely to get into a fight with whatever is threatening us; some of us will be more inclined to run away, while others may freeze.

The drive system is what gets us out of bed in the morning and off to work to provide for ourselves and our loved ones. This system is focused on getting the resources that we need to survive and thrive in the world. We experience drive to get things done, to achieve our goals and we may feel excitement as we move towards these goals.

The soothing system is connected with feelings of safeness, contentment and connection with others. This system can only operate when there are no threats to our safety and when we have sufficient resources for the time being. When this system is activated we are able to soothe ourselves in times of difficulty, to approach another for support and it enables us to feel safe.

All three systems are important for our survival and well-being. For example, if we step out in front of a bus, it's vital that the threat system activates so we immediately step back. We need the drive system to gather resources required to live and prosper in the world. The soothing system is involved in our need to have some downtime to rest, relax and connect with our loved ones.

Problems arise when these three systems get out of balance with each other. Let's do an exercise to get a sense of how well balanced these 3 systems are in you:

Three Circle Exercise

Find a large piece of paper and draw the three circles (as shown in the diagram above) as they correspond to where you spend most of your time and energy. If, for example, most of your time is spent worrying and ruminating, then draw a big circle for the threat system; if you spend very little time feeling safe and contented, then draw a small circle for the soothing system etc. Once you have done this then we can move on to the second part of the exercise.

Let's begin with the threat system. Think about the things in your life right now that trigger your threat system. It may be small things, such as needing to get to work on time, concerns about the traffic, completing a piece of work; or it might be more serious things, such as facing a divorce or a worrying health problem. Write these things in your circle. Think about how much of your time is spent in this emotional system and how often these worries and concerns ripple through you.

Now pause for a bit and then focus on the things in your life that give you a sense of pleasure and enjoyment: things you feel excited about and look forward to. This could be something you want to achieve or it might be the thought of going on a holiday; it might be looking forward to coming home to a nice meal, going to the movies, or doing a good piece of work. The key thing is the experience of being energised by whatever it is, bearing in mind that some energisers can be threat focused. For example, you may want to achieve something, not because you find it enjoyable, but because you are frightened that if you do not achieve whatever it is, people might reject you. Strictly speaking this would not fall into the drive system but the threat system circle. How much time do you spend in the drive system?

Now pause for a bit and then focus on the things in your life that give you a sense of slowing down, being content and feeling a sense of well-being; not wanting to achieve anything or go anywhere, because you are content with the way things are right now. What things, activities or relationships in your life foster this sense of feeling safe, connected and content? How much time do you spend in the soothing system?

When you have completed this task, stand back and think about which system you spend most of your time in. It's not unusual for people to realise that it's the threat or drive system.

If our three circles are a bit out of balance, it is best not to take this personally. It is not our fault. We live in a world that promotes threat. There are many subtle messages in the media telling us that we are not thin enough, attractive enough or clever enough. There is a lot of news on the television and in the newspapers about terrible things happening locally and all around the world. There are many newspapers, which are full of critical and judgmental articles, and there are many TV programmes, which go looking for people with problems, so as to humiliate them for our pleasure. Many of us spend our time watching movies and playing computer games in which people are killing and maiming each other with ever-increasing cruelty and gore. We are constantly being told about the difficult economic situation, so that many of us live in fear of losing our livelihood, our homes and the safety and security of our families. It is no wonder that we don't feel safe in the world and that our threat system is in overdrive.

Furthermore, in our Western capitalist culture the overwhelming priority is to achieve success in terms of power and money. We are constantly receiving messages from advertising that we need to buy lots of things to make us feel better and improve our status. The marketing companies that make the adverts are well aware of our drive systems and how to stimulate them.

With our 24-hour, 7 day a week culture, people are working longer hours and all the adults in the family generally have to work to support the family. When we are not working we are constantly seeking stimulation from the ever-burgeoning entertainment industry. Our society values activity and achievement and very little value is given to simply doing nothing. The culture we live in does little to promote or value the soothing/contentment system.

This means that for a lot of us the drive and threat systems are overstimulated and the soothing/contentment is under-stimulated. The brain rewires itself accordingly and so we live our lives anxious, worried, fearful, overworked and stressed out. This prevents us from making it a priority to take care of ourselves, our loved ones or the natural environment. There is little space left for relaxation and to spend time with our loved ones.

The overstimulated threat system gives rise to stress. Stress is a beneficial coping strategy to survive. There is nothing wrong with stress, but we need to take enough time to recover and regenerate. If we make an emergency out of every situation, the body reacts by producing adrenaline and this stops us from feeling tired, so we keep going, not realising what a large amount of energy we are asking from our bodies. We use drugs like caffeine and alcohol, and this leads to burnout, which is becoming more and more common in modern life.

If we spend our lives constantly stressed out, it is not helpful to blame ourselves for this. We live in a society full of people living like this and in a society that promotes this as the right way to be. The important thing with the exercise we just did is to notice where the imbalances lie, and to gradually shift our priorities. In all likelihood this will mean creating conditions in our lives that foster safeness, contentment and connection – the key elements of the soothing system. When we do this both our Mindfulness and self-compassion practices will begin to flourish.

Something else to bear in mind is that the evolved brain is very tricky. It is not designed for happiness and contentment. The threat system evolved for dealing with external threats, but we have evolved an awareness that gives rise to a sense of self-identity. This enables us to generate self-created internal threats. We can think about and give meaning to our thoughts and feelings. We can imagine all sorts of threats to ourselves and our loved ones. We can worry about the future and bring to mind painful memories. This is exacerbated if we are self-critical. All of this activity within the human mind can activate our threat system and cause lots of suffering. Most of the time we are not even aware that we are doing this; we just live with an overactivated threat system and think that this is normal.

Think for a minute or so about your favourite meal. Close your eyes and imagine how it looks? Imagine how it smells and tastes and notice what happens. Now write down here what you noticed during your reflection:

_____

_____

_____

This exercise can show the power of our imaginations. Often when we think about our favourite meal a physical reaction occurs and the mouth begins to water. In the same way, worrying about imagined futures or dwelling on bad memories can activate our threat system. A physical reaction occurs and we feel anxiety, anger, sadness – as if we were living the imagined future or remembered past right now. Similarly, when we are kind to ourselves and practise self-compassion, we activate the soothing system and stimulate hormones like oxytocin and endorphins that enhance our sense of well-being.

For all these reasons we have a tricky brain, and we are stuck with it! We can let ourselves off the hook if we think we are neurotic. It is the human condition. Our first act of self-compassion is to let go of blame for how we are. We start where we are by coming to terms with how we are. Once we do this we can take responsibility for our lives and begin to move forward in a mature and realistic way.

Practice Schedule for the Week after Session Seven

Formal Practice

Alternate the RAIN practice with the bodyscan or mindful movement. You can use the guided audio from the MBLC app or on the webpage listed on page 6. When doing the RAIN practice, if there is no difficulty present, then bring to mind a minor difficulty and practise with that. At the end, reflect on what happened during your period of practice and make notes below. In particular, write down what you noticed about how you were relating to the difficulty in the RAIN practice.

Day 1

_____

_____

_____

Day 2

_____

_____

_____

Day 3

_____

_____

_____

Day 4

_____

_____

_____

Day 5

_____

_____

_____

Day 6

_____

_____

_____

Day 7

_____

_____

_____

Informal Daily Life Practice

Continue with your previous daily life activities and again add another one. Write here what your new daily life activity is going to be:

_____

_____

Do the three stage breathing space three times a day whenever appropriate and in particular when you experience moments of happiness. Do the self-compassion break when difficulties arise in daily life or in your practice.

Describe below what you noticed when doing your informal daily life practice:

Day 1

_____

_____

_____

Day 2

_____

_____

_____

Day 3

_____

_____

_____

Day 4

_____

_____

Day 5

_____

_____

Day 6

_____

_____

Day 7

_____

_____

Chapter 9

Session Eight – A Mindfulness Based Life

Mindfulness Support Revisited

As we come to the end of this course it may be useful to look again at how we are relating to our Mindfulness support. When we start our Mindfulness practice we often cling on to the support 'for dear life', as though we were grasping a pebble tightly in our hand. As our practice matures, however, we begin to understand that genuine practice is a process of moving between distraction and mindful awareness, and we accept the fact that our mind is often inclined to move away from the present moment, like a monkey jumping from branch to branch in a tree. We don't try to control or suppress the monkey, as we will have realised by now that this does not work. Instead we let the monkey go free, while at the same time patiently bringing our attention back to the Mindfulness support again and again. When we do this the monkey gradually begins to settle. When we begin to experience this in our practice we are able to loosen our tight grip on the Mindfulness support – allowing the pebble to rest upon our open hand.

In this way, we learn to relate to our Mindfulness support with a 'feather-light touch'. A small proportion of our focus is on the support, while the rest of our attention is open and aware, noticing whatever is arising within our experience. It is as though we were looking at an object with a tight focus and then relaxing our eyes so we could see not only the object, but also the field of view surrounding it. What builds this capacity is maintaining grounding and resting as the foundation of our Mindfulness practice. This is something that we explored in Chapter 4. Whenever we get distracted we gently refocus our attention on the support and come back to where we are: body resting on the ground, mind resting in the body: we always come back to the grounding and resting. Our rule of thumb was 20% focus on the Mindfulness support and 80% awareness of grounding and resting. This is an important principle to bear in mind as we practise, because it facilitates the 'feather-light touch'. In order to get a felt sense of how to relate lightly to the Mindfulness support, let's have a go at the next exercise.

Mindfulness Support Revisited Exercise

Follow the exercise written out below or follow the guided audio on the webpage listed on page 6 or adapt the SGRS with breath exercise on the MBLC app.

Do this exercise for around 20 minutes.

Follow the normal routine of intention, motivation, settling, grounding, resting and Mindfulness support using breath as the support.

Now place one hand in front of your body with the palm facing down and each time you breathe in, lift the hand to chest level and each time you breathe out lower the hand to belly level. Allow the movement of the hand to follow the movement of the breath, so that each time an in-breath begins the hand begins to move up and each time an out-breath begins the hand begins to move down. Now rest the forefinger of the other hand on the back of the hand that is moving. Allow the finger to follow the movement of the hand, keeping the lightest of touches between the tip of the forefinger and the back of the hand.

Notice that as you do this you are simultaneously able to feel the touch between the finger and hand as well as the movement of the breath in the body. Notice how you are also able to open up to the whole of your experience – sights, sounds, and activity within the mind – while still maintaining a light focus on the feeling of touch between the finger and the hand. Do this for a few minutes.

Now place your hands down and follow the movement of the breath with the same lightness of touch that you had between the finger and the hand. Notice how you are able to simultaneously follow the breath and open up to all of your experience in this moment.

Notice how your mind moves and become curious as to where your attention goes. Wherever your mind wanders to becomes part of the practice. With this comes a sense of relaxing, opening and allowing.

As your awareness deepens you may notice that when you get distracted, your mind contracts and 'zooms in' to a thought or storyline. Noticing this, your awareness sharpens and your attention 'zooms out' again, bringing you back into your body, resting lightly with the breath in this time and place. In this way become familiar with your own unique styles of distraction and pathways of habit, and how they affect your attention.

Notice if you feel a sense of striving and let go of any sense of succeeding or failing in your practice. Let go of any sense of having to be in control. Lightly focus on the breath and casually notice how your experience is unfolding moment-by-moment.

All the time simply pay attention to what is happening while it is happening, with a kind and non-judgmental attitude.

Review of the Journey So Far

As we approach the end of this course, it is useful to reflect on what our experience of Mindfulness practice has been and how we might like to use our Mindfulness practice as a basis for living a Mindfulness Based Life.

Follow the exercise written out below and make notes in the spaces provided.

Begin by going through the normal routine of intention, motivation, settling, grounding, resting and Mindfulness support using breath as the support.

Spend some time reflecting on the following questions and write whatever comes to mind in the space provided. You might like to do this several times and see what emerges.

How was I when I started the first session of this course?

_____

_____

_____

How am I now after following the course and its practices?

_____

_____

_____

What are the main things I have learned on this course?

_____

_____

_____

How will I implement what I have learned into my daily life?

_____

_____

_____

What are my reasons for continuing to practise Mindfulness after this course ends?

_____

_____

_____

Realistically how many minutes per day do I want to commit to my daily formal Mindfulness practice?

_____

_____

_____

Which of the formal practices covered on this course would I like to do on a regular basis? (eg: sitting practice, bodyscan, mindful movement, loving kindness practice)

_____

_____

_____

Which of the daily life practices covered on this course would I like to do on a regular basis? (eg: breathing space, compassion break, daily life activities)

_____

What will I say to myself if I experience a resistance to continuing to practise Mindfulness (eg: Nike slogan – Just do it!)

Chapter 10

The Rest of Your Life

In Chapter 9 we reflected on what it means to live a Mindfulness based life, and in particular which formal and informal practices we wanted to do. We also reflected on why we wanted to do these practices and what we might do if we experienced resistance to practising them. Now we will take some time to reflect on how our practice has been going.

Reflection on Home Practice

Do this reflection a month or so after reading Chapter 9.
Follow the exercise written out below and make notes in the spaces provided.

Begin by going through the normal routine of intention, motivation, settling, grounding, resting and Mindfulness support, using breath as the support.

Spend some time reflecting on the following questions and write whatever comes to mind in the space provided. You might like to do this several times and see what emerges.

How has my home practice been going over the last month?

_____

_____

_____

Which practices have I been doing?

_____

_____

_____

What have I been noticing in my Mindfulness practice?

_____

_____

_____

Now compare what you have written above to your reflection in Chapter 9. Don't waste any time or energy in beating yourself up if you have not practised as much as you had intended. Instead spend some time reflecting again on your motivation: Why do you want to practise Mindfulness in your life? How will this benefit yourself and those around you.

What Comes Next?

It can be very supportive to practise Mindfulness as part of a group. Many of our course participants comment how motivating it is to be part of a group of practitioners that come together and practise regularly. In the Buddhist tradition there is a lot of focus on *sangha* or spiritual community: being part of a group of like-minded people, who hold similar values and who practise together. These days there are some secular *sanghas* as well as Buddhist ones. It might be useful to seek out a practice group that is near to you and whose values resonate with your own, and consider practising with this group on a regular basis.

Finding an MBLC Teacher

It is also very helpful to have a teacher or mentor. You may be able to find a Mindfulness Based Living Course (MBLC) teacher locally, but make sure that they are properly qualified by ensuring that they are trained and that they practise according to the UK Good Practice Guidelines for Mindfulness Teachers. For more details see http://mindfulnessteachersuk.org.uk/. This website includes a listing of Mindfulness Based Living Course (MBLC) teachers that meet these guidelines. On the listing page of this website select MBLC from the drop down box.

Mindfulness Association Courses

The Mindfulness Association, which was founded by the authors of this book, is a listed organisation within the UK Network for Mindfulness Teachers and trains teachers according to the UK Good Practice Guidelines. For information about the ongoing work of the Mindfulness Association and the range of courses that it offers, please visit the website: www.mindfulnessassociation. net.

If you would like to attend a Mindfulness course with the Mindfulness Association it runs a four-weekend Level 1 Mindfulness course: Being Present, in several locations across the UK and in some European countries.

After the Mindfulness course, a Level 2 Mindfulness Course: Responding with Compassion is offered, and after this, a Level 3 Mindfulness Course: Seeing Deeply.

In addition the Mindfulness Association provides a two-year Mindfulness teacher training pathway, which includes the four-weekend Level 1 Mindfulness course, two weekends of Introductory teaching skills, plus a 5-day Mindfulness Based Living Course retreat. Successful completion of this pathway enables you to be listed on the UK listing of Mindfulness teachers.

There are many free resources available on the resources page of the Mindfulness Association website, including video and audio talks.

We also offer a range of online courses, all of which include regular live training with Mindfulness Association tutors.

For more information about any of the above, please contact MAHQ by emailing:

info@mindfulnessassociation.net

Master's Degree in Studies in Mindfulness at the University of Aberdeen

The Mindfulness Association works in partnership with the University of Aberdeen in the delivery of this Masters Degree course. Both Heather and Choden teach on the MSc. For more information please see: https://www.mindfulnessassociation.net/msc

Mindfulness Association Membership

The Mindfulness Association has an online membership that you can join. This provides a variety of benefits including weekly live online guided practices, monthly live online teachings, access to audio guided practices, as well as audio and video teachings from its annual conferences, and a quarterly newsletter. These resources are designed to support a regular and effective Mindfulness practice.

Details can be found on the resources page of the website: www.mindfulnessassociation.net.

In order to join you will need to agree to the Mindfulness Association Membership Pledge.

Mindfulness Association Membership Pledge

On joining the Mindfulness Association's (MA's) Membership and on renewing your annual Membership, you agree to the following:

1. I have or intend to have a daily Mindfulness practice.

2. I intend to embody Mindfulness and Compassion as core values in my life.

3. I will be kind and respectful to the other members of the Membership in my online communications with them.

Recommended Reading

We can recommend the following books:

Diamond Mind by Rob Nairn, who is the Founder of the Mindfulness Association.

Mindful Compassion by Professor Paul Gilbert and Choden. Professor Gilbert is a patron of the Mindfulness Association and Choden is a Director of the Mindfulness Association, as well as a co-author of this book.

Chapter 11

Mindfulness Skills for Times of Difficulty

Sometimes there are periods in our lives that are full of difficulties, such as bereavement, illness, redundancy, relationship endings or divorce, overwork and other life stresses. During these times our mood may be lower than usual.

Also, when our mindfulness practice strengthens we can become aware of deeply embedded patterns of thoughts and behaviour, which were often established in our childhood or youth. These deeper habit patterns can be difficult to face and come to terms with, and as we go through the process of accepting them, which may take some time, the emotions that arise may be overwhelming. It is beneficial to go through this process of acceptance because it results in the growth of our wisdom and compassion, but it can lower our mood and make our lives more challenging.

If you have recently suffered a difficult life event or if your mindfulness practice is opening up difficulties from earlier in your life, then the wise course of action may be to reduce or stop your mindfulness practice for a while.

Also, if you are going through a sustained period of low mood, consider visiting your GP for help or consulting an evidence-based psychological therapy practitioner such as cognitive behavioural therapy (CBT).

Furthermore, there are strategies which we can be put in place to more skilfully navigate our way through such difficult times and periods of low mood.

Formal Practice

Over the course of this training there are home practice assignments and these require you to do a daily practice of around 30 minutes. In times of difficulty it is not uncommon to find that you are regularly becoming overwhelmed by emotions when you do your formal practice. If this happens and you find that it is lowering your mood in your daily life or making life more difficult, then experiment with the following options:

- Use the RAIN exercise to help you come to terms with the emotions you are experiencing. If you still feel overwhelmed, it may be unkind to yourself to continue to sit in a state of overwhelm. Here we work the 'edge' between approaching and staying with the difficulty on the one hand and withdrawing from the difficulty on the other hand. Only you can determine where this 'edge' lies in your own practice, and it will be different from one day to the next. But if your practice is causing your mood to drop, this may be a sign that you are pushing too hard at the 'edge'. To pull back from the 'edge', first acknowledge the difficulty you are experiencing and commit to addressing the difficulty in future mindfulness practice (this helps to avoid suppression of the difficulty); then get up and do an enjoyable activity that will distract you from the difficulty;
- Sit for shorter periods of time, for example 10 or 15 minutes, once or twice a day;
- Switch to doing a mindfulness practice that nourishes or soothes you and which is less overwhelming. For example, you may find that switching to mindful movement, bodyscan, loving kindness practice or mindful walking (through the park or in the countryside) is more beneficial;
- Have a few days off from your formal practice and carry on with your informal practice, such as the three stage breathing space, self-compassion break and mindful daily life activities.

Increasing Awareness of Pleasant Events

Even in the most difficult of times, there are pleasant moments to be experienced. Our minds have evolved to attend to and remember threatening situations as a means of survival. As Rick Hanson says, unpleasant events can stick to the mind like Velcro while pleasant events can slide off the mind like silk. This natural tendency can be reinforced by our mindfulness practice in daily life in which we practise becoming present when a difficult situation arises, so as to create space to respond skilfully rather than reacting automatically. To counteract this tendency to focus on unpleasant events, we practise attending to pleasant events in our daily life. The pleasant event might be anything from sipping a nice cup of tea, to feeling the sun on your face, or to seeing a child at play.

When we encounter difficulties in life or low mood, one approach is to attend more closely to pleasant events. In order to do this, we can use the pleasant events calendar below. In daily life we can have the intention to become aware of at least one pleasant event every day while the event is happening. Then later we can fill out the details of the event in the pleasant events calendar. By living our lives with the intention to become mindful of pleasant events, we gradually develop the habit of becoming more aware during the pleasant moments in our day. This enables us to deeply experience the pleasant events in our lives and the thoughts, physical sensations and emotions that go along with them.

Pleasant Events Calendar

	Example	Day/date	Day/date	Day/date
What was the experience?	Meeting a good friend while shopping who I hadn't heard from in a long time			
Were you aware of the pleasant feelings while the event was happening?	Yes			
What sensations did you experience in the body during the experience?	Smiling across mouth; aware of some excitement in the chest; a lot of energy in the body			
What moods, feelings and thoughts accompanied the event?	Surprise and mild excitement at speaking to her; felt happy talking to her again			
What's in your mind now as you write this down?	It was a short meeting and I'm surprised how good it made me feel to see her			

Adapted from *Full Catastrophe Living* by Jon Kabat-Zinn

Nourishing and Depleting Activities

Depleting activities are activities that we do in our daily life which drain our energy and lower our mood, such as frustrating or repetitive aspects of our job, staying up too late, drinking too much alcohol, getting stuck in traffic or conversations with particular people.

Nourishing activities are activities that we do in our life which give us pleasure, boost our energy and improve our mood, such as taking a nice long bath, going out with a friend, going for a walk, listening to music or watching an uplifting movie or TV programme. Nourishing activities also include activities which give us a sense of accomplishment or mastery because we are getting things done; for example by finishing a task we have been avoiding doing, like doing the housework or writing a letter. Think back and remember if there are any activities that you used to do which nourished you.

Take time to reflect over the activities you do in your daily life and place each activity in the appropriate column in the table below. Be specific and detailed about these activities.

Depleting Activities	Nourishing Activities

Adapted from *Mindfulness-Based Cognitive Therapy for Depression* by Segal, Williams and Teasdale

Then once you have completed your list, take steps to reduce the number of depleting activities you engage with in your daily life. You may not be able to avoid some of the depleting activities, so think about how you can change the way you engage in these activities so as to make them less depleting.

For example, if you have an activity that depletes you and which you cannot avoid, then you could perhaps try one of the following options:

- make that activity one of your mindfulness practices by staying mindful as you do it;
- commit to get the activity done first thing in the morning or straight away, so that you are not anticipating it all day;
- break the activity up into manageable chunks interspersed with more enjoyable activities;
- contemplate any beneficial results that arise from completing this activity to make it more meaningful.

In this way try to be creative in developing strategies to reduce or change the way you engage in depleting activities.

Also, schedule into your day more nourishing activities. You can start by adding one or two new nourishing activities and then gradually add more. Again, be creative in how you do this.

BOOKS

O-BOOKS

SPIRITUALITY

O is a symbol of the world, of oneness and unity; this eye represents knowledge and insight. We publish titles on general spirituality and living a spiritual life. We aim to inform and help you on your own journey in this life.

If you have enjoyed this book, why not tell other readers by posting a review on your preferred book site? Recent bestsellers from O-Books are:

Heart of Tantric Sex
Diana Richardson
Revealing Eastern secrets of deep love and intimacy to Western couples.
Paperback: 978-1-90381-637-0 ebook: 978-1-84694-637-0

Crystal Prescriptions
The A-Z guide to over 1,200 symptoms and their healing crystals
Judy Hall
The first in the popular series of six books, this handy little guide is packed as tight as a pill-bottle with crystal remedies for ailments.
Paperback: 978-1-90504-740-6 ebook: 978-1-84694-629-5

Take Me To Truth
Undoing the Ego
Nouk Sanchez, Tomas Vieira
The best-selling step-by-step book on shedding the Ego, using the teachings of *A Course In Miracles*.
Paperback: 978-1-84694-050-7 ebook: 978-1-84694-654-7

The 7 Myths about Love...Actually!
The journey from your HEAD to the HEART of your SOUL
Mike George
Smashes all the myths about LOVE.
Paperback: 978-1-84694-288-4 ebook: 978-1-84694-682-0

The Holy Spirit's Interpretation of the New Testament
A course in Understanding and Acceptance
Regina Dawn Akers
Following on from the strength of *A Course In Miracles*, NTI teaches us how to experience the love and oneness of God.
Paperback: 978-1-84694-085-9 ebook: 978-1-78099-083-5

The Message of A Course In Miracles
A translation of the text in plain language
Elizabeth A. Cronkhite
A translation of *A Course in Miracles* into plain, everyday language for anyone seeking inner peace. The companion volume, *Practicing A Course In Miracles*, offers practical lessons and mentoring.
Paperback: 978-1-84694-319-5 ebook: 978-1-84694-642-4

Thinker's Guide to God
Peter Vardy
An introduction to key issues in the philosophy of religion.
Paperback: 978-1-90381-622-6

Your Simple Path
Find happiness in every step
Ian Tucker
A guide to helping us reconnect with what is really important in our lives.
Paperback: 978-1-78279-349-6 ebook: 978-1-78279-348-9

365 Days of Wisdom
Daily Messages To Inspire You Through The Year
Dadi Janki
Daily messages which cool the mind, warm the heart and guide you along your journey.
Paperback: 978-1-84694-863-3 ebook: 978-1-84694-864-0

Body of Wisdom
Women's Spiritual Power and How it Serves
Hilary Hart
Bringing together the dreams and experiences of women across the world with today's most visionary spiritual teachers.
Paperback: 978-1-78099-696-7 ebook: 978-1-78099-695-0

Dying to Be Free
From Enforced Secrecy to Near Death to True Transformation
Hannah Robinson
After an unexpected accident and near-death experience, Hannah Robinson found herself radically transforming her life, while a remarkable new insight altered her relationship with her father, a practising Catholic priest.
Paperback: 978-1-78535-254-6 ebook: 978-1-78535-255-3

The Ecology of the Soul
A Manual of Peace, Power and Personal Growth for Real People
in the Real World
Aidan Walker
Balance your own inner Ecology of the Soul to regain your
natural state of peace, power and wellbeing.
Paperback: 978-1-78279-850-7 ebook: 978-1-78279-849-1

Not I, Not other than I
The Life and Teachings of Russel Williams
Steve Taylor, Russel Williams
The miraculous life and inspiring teachings of one of the World's
greatest living Sages.
Paperback: 978-1-78279-729-6 ebook: 978-1-78279-728-9

On the Other Side of Love
A Woman's Unconventional Journey Towards Wisdom
Muriel Maufroy
When life has lost all meaning, what do you do?
Paperback: 978-1-78535-281-2 ebook: 978-1-78535-282-9

Practicing A Course In Miracles
A Translation of the Workbook in Plain Language and With
Mentoring Notes
Elizabeth A. Cronkhite
The practical second and third volumes of The Plain-Language
A Course In Miracles.
Paperback: 978-1-84694-403-1 ebook: 978-1-78099-072-9

Quantum Bliss

The Quantum Mechanics of Happiness, Abundance, and Health

George S. Mentz

Quantum Bliss is the breakthrough summary of success and spirituality secrets that customers have been waiting for.

Paperback: 978-1-78535-203-4 ebook: 978-1-78535-204-1

The Upside Down Mountain

Mags MacKean

A must-read for anyone weary of chasing success and happiness – one woman's inspirational journey swapping the uphill slog for the downhill slope.

Paperback: 978-1-78535-171-6 ebook: 978-1-78535-172-3

Your Personal Tuning Fork

The Endocrine System

Deborah Bates

Discover your body's health secret, the endocrine system, and 'twang' your way to sustainable health!

Paperback: 978-1-84694-503-8 ebook: 978-1-78099-697-4

Readers of ebooks can buy or view any of these bestsellers by clicking on the live link in the title. Most titles are published in paperback and as an ebook. Paperbacks are available in traditional bookshops. Both print and ebook formats are available online.

Find more titles and sign up to our readers' newsletter at http://www.johnhuntpublishing.com/mind-body-spirit

Follow us on Facebook at https://www.facebook.com/OBooks/ and Twitter at https://twitter.com/obooks